CZECH REPUBLIC

- A ☑ in the text denotes a highly recommended sight
- A complete A–Z of practical information starts on p.115
- Extensive mapping throughout: on cover flaps and in text

Copyright © **1996** by Berlitz Publishing Co. Ltd, Berlitz House, Peterley Road, Oxford OX4 2TX, England, and Berlitz Publishing Company, Inc., 257 Park Avenue South, New York, NY 10010, USA.

Printed in Switzerland by Weber SA, Bienne.

1st edition (1996)

Although we make every effort to ensure the accuracy of the information in this guide, changes do occur. If you have any new information, suggestions or corrections to contribute to the guide, we would like to hear from you. Please write to Berlitz Publishing at one of the above addresses.

Text:	Neil Wilson
Editor:	Renée Ferguson, Brigitte Lee
Photography:	Neil Wilson
Layout:	Suzanna Boyle, Paula Wilson
Cartography:	Visual Image
Thanks to:	The Czech Tourist Authority for their help in producing this guide

Cover photograph: *Český Krumlov*
Photograph on page 4: *Vyšší Brod Monastery, South Bohemia*

CONTENTS

The Country and the People

'Good King Wenceslas looked out, on the feast of Stephen…' We all know the old Christmas carol, but how many of us know that the land he looked out over was the kingdom of Bohemia? Wenceslas was the pious 10th-century prince of an ancient realm that today, with its neighbour Moravia, lies within the borders of the modern Czech Republic. At the crossroads of Europe, this small but resilient nation has managed to maintain its own identity through centuries of war, repression and imperial domination, to emerge in the 1990s as one of the most confident and prosperous of the former Warsaw Pact countries.

The Czech Republic covers an area of some 78,700 sq km (30,400 sq miles), about the same size as Scotland or South Carolina, and encompasses the ancient Czech Lands of Bohemia and Moravia. It is at the geographical heart of Europe, sharing borders with Germany to the west, Austria to the south, Slovakia to the east, and Poland to the north. These are natural borders, defined by ranges of hills that enclose two major river basins: to the west, the Bohemian basin is drained by the rivers Vltava and Labe (Elbe), which join and flow north into Germany and thence to the North Sea, while the Morava river in the east carries the waters of the Moravian basin south to merge with the Danube and, eventually, the Black Sea.

The mountains that ring the republic are rich in minerals, a resource that the Czechs have exploited profitably for many centuries. The medieval silver mines of Kutná Hora ensured Bohemia's status as one of the richest kingdoms in Europe in the 14th century – the Prague *groš* was then quite possibly the continent's most stable currency. Graphite dug from the hills of South Bohemia has, since the 19th century, been exported around the world as the 'lead' used in the well-known *Koh-i-noor* brand **5** pencils. But more importantly, the coal mines of Chomutov and Ostrava, and the lead, zinc and tin of the Jeseníky mountains and Krušné hory (literally, the 'Ore Mountains'), were to a large extent responsible for the region's development as the thriving industrial heartland of the late 19th-century Austro-Hungarian Empire.

Bohemia's industrial legacy has created some of the worst environmental damage in the whole of central Europe – a landscape scarred with open-cast coal pits, rivers black with pollution, and forests ruined by acid rain. The damage is fortunately restricted to North Bohemia, along the country's borders with eastern Germany and Poland. Elsewhere the Czech landscape is a pleasing patchwork of green fields and forests, laced with rivers and dotted with charming towns.

The main attraction for visitors to the Czech Republic is its vast wealth of historical and architectural treasures. Gothic churches, Renaissance castles and Baroque palaces abound, not only in the capital, Prague, but also among the pine-clad hills, and the towns and cities that have managed to preserve their medieval cores largely unspoilt. Foreign investment has enabled vital renovation work to continue, and many of the country's historic buildings have been splendidly restored. In a land that boasts nearly 1,800 castles, the biggest difficulty for the visitor is where to start. Some of the finest examples can be found within easy reach of Prague, for example

*M*usic making is second nature to the Czechs, whether it's **6** folk, jazz or classical.

Charles IV's royal retreat at Karlštejn, or the Habsburg hunting lodge of Archduke Franz Ferdinand at Konopiště. Further afield, you can wander through the stately wood-panelled halls of Bouzov Castle, seat of the Grand Masters of the Teutonic Knights, or be dazzled by the opulence of Vranov Castle, a Baroque masterpiece perched on top of a cliff in the southern fringes of Moravia. In the west, some of the country's most attractive 19th-century architecture can be admired in the renowned spa towns of Mariánské Lázně, Františkovy Lázně and Karlovy Vary.

Although a good deal of the Czech landscape is gentle and pastoral – making it popular with cyclists – there are places where nature has sculpted the hard Bohemian bedrock into a series of scenic wonders. Wind and water have whittled the sandstone cliffs of North and East Bohemia into a wonderland of fluted pinnacles and precipitous gorges, while the limestone plateau of the Moravian Karst has been dissolved

Fine Baroque buildings grace many Czech towns and cities – this is the Loretto in Prague.

and dissected by subterranean streams to produce an echoing underworld of stalagmites and stalactites. These more remote regions are popular arenas for various outdoor sports, from hikers pursuing the forest trails of the Šumava, or canoeists exploring the upper reaches of the Vltava and Otava rivers, to rock climbers clinging to the crags of Adršpach-Teplice, **7** and skiers slaloming their way through the winter snows of the Krkonoše mountains.

The Czech Republic's greatest and most famous treasure is, of course, Prague. Thought of as one of Europe's most beautiful and romantic cities, the Czech capital is a fantasy of wedding-cake palaces and pinnacled, Gothic spires mirrored in the dreamy waters of the Vltava. You can lose yourself in its maze of medieval streets, now lined with antique shops and beer cellars, or take in a broader view from a park bench on Petřín Hill. A cruise along the river and dinner in a traditional restaurant can be followed by an unforgettable night at the opera or concert hall. The city's great cultural tradition draws thousands of tourists each year to enjoy performances of classical music by the Czech Philharmonic

The wooded hills and forests of Bohemia provide a welcome contrast to the bustle of the cities.

8

and other orchestras – this is, after all, the city that nurtured the talents of Dvořák, Smetana and Janáček, and hosted the world premieres of Mozart's *Don Giovanni* and Mahler's Seventh Symphony. Berlioz, Beethoven, Paganini, Wagner, Tchaikovsky and Liszt also performed here.

The capital accounts for just over one tenth of the country's population of 10.5 million, of whom 95% are Czech and 3% Slovak, with small minorities of Polish, German, Hungarian and Romany (Gypsy) extraction. As one of the few Eastern Bloc countries with a strong democratic tradition, Czech people are individualistic and independent-minded, but they retain a strong, old-fashioned streak of courtesy and good

manners. It is not at all unusual to see a long-haired youth in heavy-metal T-shirt and torn jeans give up his seat on the train to an elderly citizen, and fortunately the old tradition of hospitality towards travellers is still extended to today's visitors. The Czechs' strong sense of national identity springs in no small way from the Czech language, a Slavic tongue with an ancient pedigree, which is closely related to Slovak and Polish. As a literary language, it can trace its origins to the 14th century, when the court of the Přemysl kings produced a significant quantity of epic poems, dramas, histories and religious writings.

Writers have always played an important part throughout Czech history, from the religious reformer Jan Hus in the 15th century to the country's present playwright-president, Václav Havel. Perhaps the Czechs' best-known and best-loved fictional character is *The Good Soldier Švejk*, created by Jaroslav Hašek in the 1920s. Švejk is an amiable malingerer who manages to bamboozle every official who persecutes him. His riotous adventures in the Austrian army during World War I cunningly satirize Habsburg bureaucracy and the absurdities of war. Among other Czech writers who have made their names abroad are Franz Kafka (who wrote in German), Ivan Klíma and Milan Kundera.

You can drink a toast to Švejk in one of the beer halls that were the wily soldier's frequent haunt. You can even visit Švejk's favourite pub, where the opening scenes of the novel are set – *U Kalicha* (The Chalice), in Prague's Nové Město, is still open for business, though it is now a busy tourist restaurant. Czech beer is justly renowned as the world's best – in fact it was here, in the city of Plzeň, that Pilsner lager was invented in the 13th century, and where the original, Pilsner Urquell, is still brewed today.

So why not raise your glass to Švejk, to Czech beer, and to one of Europe's newest and most fascinating countries – *Na zdraví*!

A Brief History

The Czech Republic is one of the world's youngest states. It was born on 1 January 1993, when it formally parted from its neighbour and long-time partner Slovakia, in what has inevitably come to be known as the Velvet Divorce. But the Czech Lands, comprising the old kingdoms of Bohemia and Moravia, have a long and often fascinating history, and they have played a pivotal role in the development of Europe – both ancient and modern.

In prehistoric times the Czech Lands were inhabited by Celtic tribes, one of them being the Boii, from which the name Bohemia is derived. The early Celts were followed by Germanic tribes, until they themselves were displaced by Slavic settlers from the east in the 5th and 6th centuries AD.

*S*t Wenceslas, the patron saint of the Czech Republic, watches over central Prague.

One of the Slavic tribes, the Czechs (named, so it is said, after a chieftain called Čech), established themselves among the forests and hills of central Bohemia. But it was the Slavs of the neighbouring Morava river basin to the east who first rose to prominence.

Having been granted land by Charlemagne for helping him defeat the Avars of Hungary, the Moravian tribes were

united under Prince Mojmír to form the short-lived Great Moravian Empire (830-906). Mojmír's successor, Rostislav, was responsible for inviting the Byzantine emperor to send his Christian missionaries to preach in the Slavic language. Saints Cyril and Methodius arrived in 863, and not only preached but also translated many sacred texts, inventing a Slavic (Cyrillic) alphabet as they did so. The empire, which had encompassed Moravia, Bohemia, and parts of Germany, Poland, Slovakia and Hungary, soon succumbed to invasion by the Franks and Magyars, and by the beginning of the 10th century it had ceased to exist.

The Princess and the Ploughboy

The first Czech dynasty was descended from the legendary Princess Libuše, who founded the city of Prague. Tradition maintains that she married a local ploughman, and their offspring were the first in the line of Přemysl princes who ruled Bohemia from the 9th to the early 14th centuries. The most famous of these rulers was Prince Wenceslas (Václav in Czech), who ruled from 921 to 929, and was immortalized as 'Good King Wenceslas' in the Christmas carol of the same name. A pious man, he established a church dedicated to St Vitus on Prague's castle hill, but sadly was murdered by his ambitious brother Boleslav. He was later canonized, and became the patron saint of the Czech Lands.

The Přemysl princes ruled Bohemia and Moravia from their stronghold in Prague, under the suzerainty of the neighbouring Holy Roman Empire (comprising Germany, eastern France, and northern Italy). Castles were built and monasteries established, and during the 13th century large numbers of immigrants arrived from the overpopulated areas of Germany. The new arrivals built towns, opened mines and cleared farms, increasing the prosperity and power of the Czech Lands. In 1198, the Holy Roman Empire granted

Historical Landmarks

5th cen. AD   Slavic tribes arrive in Bohemia and Moravia.

830-906   Great Moravian Empire.

9th cen.   Founders of Přemysl dynasty build first castle at Prague.

921-929   Reign of 'Good King' Wenceslas.

1346-78   Reign of Charles IV, Bohemia's Golden Age.

1415   6 July: Jan Hus burnt at the stake.

1458-71   Reign of George of Poděbrady, Bohemia's only Hussite king.

1618   23 May: Defenestration of Prague marks beginning of the Thirty Years' War (1618-48).

1620   Hussites defeated at Battle of the White Mountain.

17th cen.   Counter-Reformation: forced re-Catholicization of Czech Lands; building of Baroque churches and palaces.

1740-80   Reign of Empress Maria Theresa; reforms introduced to Habsburg empire.

1848   Nationalist uprising in Prague, Czech National Revival.

1918   New republic of Czechoslovakia created following the break-up of the Austro-Hungarian Empire.

1939   Northern Bohemia (the Sudetenland) is annexed by Nazi Germany, marking start of World War II.

1948   Communist Party takes power and proclaims the People's Republic of Czechoslovakia.

1968   Prague Spring – Dubček's democratic experiment crushed by invasion of Soviet tanks.

1989   The Velvet Revolution leads to the collapse of communist rule; Václav Havel elected president.

1993   1 January: the Velvet Divorce sees the creation of separate Czech and Slovak republics.

failed in battle, and ruled over much of Poland and parts of Hungary. But these lands were lost after his death, and the murder of his son in Olomouc in 1306 marked the end of the Přemysl dynasty.

The Golden Age of Charles IV

Přemysl Otakar I (1197-1230) the hereditary title of King of Bohemia, and his son, Přemysl Otakar II (1253-78), expanded his domain to include parts of Austria. This provoked a war with the German king, Rudolf of Habsburg, who claimed the Austrian territory for himself, and Otakar II was brought down in battle in 1278.

His successor, Wenceslas II (1278-1305), bolstered by the vast wealth that was coming from the silver mines of Kutná Hora, succeeded with diplomacy where his father had

The Bohemian nobles elected John of Luxembourg (1310-46), son of the German king and Holy Roman Emperor, Henry VII, to succeed to the Czech crown. The kingdom subsequently passed to his son, Wenceslas, who had been brought up at the French court (where he changed his name to Charles). Whilst in France, Charles obtained an excellent education, and fostered good relations with the papacy, a liaison that led to him being elected as the Holy Roman

Emperor, Charles IV (1346-78). He was an able and intelligent leader, and during his reign Bohemia flourished, especially Prague, which was now the seat of the imperial administration.

Charles promoted the Czech language, founded a university in Prague, expanded the city by establishing the New Town, and commissioned the building of many fine monuments, including Charles Bridge and St Vitus Cathedral. Scholars, artists and architects from all over central Europe flocked to Prague, which became one of Europe's largest and most important cities. Charles also built Karlštejn Castle as a place of safe-keeping for the crown jewels, and founded the spa town of Karlovy Vary.

However, during the reign of Charles's son, Wenceslas IV (1378-1419), things began to fall apart. In 1402 Jan Hus, a scholar-priest from Prague's university, began preaching in Czech against the corruption and excesses of the Catholic Church, prefiguring Martin Luther's reform movement by almost a century. He attracted a large following of clergy, scholars and ordinary people, and although Wenceslas at first supported Hus, his continued preaching in support of reform led to his excommunication and arrest for heresy. In 1415 Hus was tried (illegally) by a papal council, denounced as a heretic, and burnt at the stake on 6 July.

Jan Žižka

Jan Žižka (1376-1424) was one of Bohemia's national heroes. A follower of the Protestant reformer Jan Hus, he became military commander of a radical Hussite community known as the Taborites. He was the inventor of mobile artillery, successfully using cannon mounted on armoured cattle wagons to defeat the forces of the Catholic king, Sigismund. It was not until 200 years later that anyone thought to copy his example.

15

A Faith Divided

Jan Hus immediately became a martyr to the Czech Reformation. The country divided into three factions: the moderate Hussites, mostly aristocrats, known as the Utraquists; the radical Hussites, for the most part peasants, known as the Taborites; and those still loyal to the Catholic Church, who were led by Sigismund (1419-37), the brother of Wenceslas IV. In 1419, a Hussite mob stormed Prague's New Town Hall and threw a number of Catholic city councillors from the window – an event that sparked off a long and bitter period of internal conflict known as the Hussite Wars. The Taborites, under Jan Žižka (see p.15), waged successful campaigns for many years from their base at Tábor, but were finally overwhelmed by a combined force of Catholics and Utraquists in 1434.

In an attempt to unite the country, the Bohemian nobles elected the Utraquist George of Poděbrady as king (1458-71), the first and last Hussite monarch to rule Bohemia. George preached religious tolerance and tried to reconcile Catholic and Hussite factions, but to no avail; he was succeeded by Vladislav Jagellonský (1471-1516), Catholic son of the Polish king.

Under the Habsburgs

When Vladislav Jagellonský's son was killed in battle against the Turks, the Bohemian throne passed to his brother-in-law, Ferdinand I of the House of Habsburg (1526-64). One of Europe's greatest sovereign dynasties, the Habsburgs were to rule the Czech Lands (as part of the Austro-Hungarian Empire) for the next 400 years. Ferdinand's grandson, Rudolf II (1575-1611), moved his imperial court from Vienna to Prague, where he escaped the problems of empire by dabbling in the arts and sciences, while slipping into madness. Prague enjoyed a cultural renaissance during his reign, but Bohemia was still racked by religious dissension as the Hussites clamoured for freedom of worship that had long been promised but never delivered.

On 23 May 1618, a crowd of Hussite nobles, enraged by Ferdinand II's attempts to impose Catholicism on Bohemia, ejected two Habsburg governors and their secretary from the window of the Chancellery in Prague Castle. The Catholic dignitaries landed in a dungheap and so escaped serious injury, but the Defenestration of Prague, as the event came to be known, marked the start of a Protestant insurrection. A Habsburg army quashed the rebels at the Battle of the White Mountain in November 1620, and the 27 Protestant nobles who had spearheaded the rebellion were executed in Prague's Old Town Square. In the backlash that inevitably ensued, Ferdinand II (1617-37) first deprived the Czechs of their rights and confiscated their property, then set about the forced re-Catholicization of Bohemia and Moravia.

As the Thirty Years' War (1618-48) tore Europe apart, the Counter-Reformation tore through Bohemia. Protestant Czech nobles emigrated, to be replaced by German-speaking Catholics; those who remained were forcibly converted to the Catholic faith. The imperial

The Habsburg Dynasty

The House of Habsburg was one of the most durable ruling dynasties of Europe. The first royal Habsburg was Rudolf I, elected king of Germany in 1273, but the family is chiefly associated with Austria, which they ruled in an unbroken line from the 15th century until 1918. During the 15th century the dynasty divided – the descendants of Charles I ruled as kings of Spain, while those of his brother Ferdinand I ruled over the Austro-Hungarian Empire. Bohemia and Moravia were Habsburg possessions from 1526 until 1918.

*M*onument to artist Karel Škréta, whose Baroque paintings adorn many Prague churches.

magnificent Baroque churches and palaces that transformed the face of Prague and other Bohemian towns in the 17th century.

During the reign of Empress Maria Theresa (1740-80), the Czech Lands suffered further damage in the wars between the Habsburg Empire and Frederick the Great of Prussia, but living conditions began to improve with the introduction of administrative reforms. Her son and heir, Josef II (1780-90), gained popular sympathy and acclaim by abolishing serfdom and granting religious freedom, and his enlightened reign paved the way for the great changes that would take place during the 19th century.

court returned to Vienna, and the huge influx of German immigrants ensured that Czech became the language of the poor and oppressed. All forms of worship other than Roman Catholicism were banned, and the spiritual triumph of the Counter-Reformation was celebrated in the building of the

National Revival

In the first half of the 19th century Bohemia was a divided society, with an aristocratic German ruling class and a poor Czech middle class and peasantry. But a small group of Czech intellectuals began to rediscover their roots, and through their books, plays and journalism succeeded in stirring a national consciousness among ordinary people, who were gradually migrating from the countryside to the towns to work in the newly developing industries. Led by the historian František Palacký, the nationalists agitated for increased self-determination, leading in June 1848 to protest and rioting in the streets of Prague.

The revolution was swiftly quashed, but the nationalist revival continued, resulting in increasing tension between the German-speaking population and the Czechs. During the long reign of Emperor Franz Josef (1830-1916), the nationalists strove to attain equal rights for the Czech Lands within the Austro-Hungarian Empire, but were vigorously opposed by the centralized Habsburg state. A new pride and interest was taken in the Czech language and traditions, reflected in the works of Czech writers and composers such as Antonín Dvořák, who took his inspiration from traditional folk songs and dances. When Prague's prestigious National Theatre was opened in 1881, the first ever performance was a patriotic opera called *Libuše*, by Czech nationalist composer Bedřich Smetana.

War and Independence

The assassination in Sarajevo of Franz Ferdinand, the heir to the Habsburg throne, in June 1914, plunged the Austro-Hungarian Empire into the awful carnage of World War I. But the Czechs and their neighbours, the Slovaks, were reluctant to fight on the same side as their Habsburg masters, especially against the Russians, whom they regarded as fellow Slavs. As the war went on Czech troops defected to the Russian side, while on the political front Tomáš Masaryk argued for a union of Czechs and Slovaks. Together with Edvard Beneš, he lobbied support for independence in the USA and among the Allied governments. The result was the proclamation of the independent Republic of Czechoslovakia on 28 October 1918, with Masaryk as its president. **19**

The new republic inherited most of the old Habsburg empire's industry, and enjoyed relative prosperity until the Great Depression of the 1930s, when the simmering resentment of the German-speaking minority (the so-called 'Sudeten Germans') was brought to the boil by Hitler's rise to power. They demanded that the Sudetenland (the largely industrial northern region of Bohemia and Moravia) should be ceded to Germany; when Hitler annexed Austria in March 1938, Czechoslovakia was thrown into turmoil. The republic's leaders looked to Britain and France for support, but in vain. The Czechs surrendered the Sudetenland, and the country was left without defences. On 16 March 1939, the German forces marched into Prague and proclaimed Bohemia and Moravia a protectorate of the Third Reich.

Although the Czech Lands sustained little material damage during Nazi occupation, the people suffered terribly. Young people were press-ganged into working for the German war economy, Czech resistance fighters were murdered in mass executions or imprisoned in concentration camps, and over 77,000 Czech Jews perished in the gas-chambers of Auschwitz, Treblinka and Majdanek. On 5 May 1945, with US troops in Plzeň, and the Soviet Red Army advancing from the east,

*T*he horrors of the Holocaust are commemorated in the graveyards of Terezín.

a popular uprising in Prague drove the remaining German forces from the city a day before the Soviet army arrived on 9 May.

The Communist Era

The independent republic of Czechoslovakia was restored, the Sudeten Germans were expelled from the country, and their towns and farms were resettled by Czechs. In the general election of 1946, the Communist Party emerged as the largest political faction, and subsequently engineered a coup d'état in 1948, prompting politicians, intellectuals and others to flee to the West.

The communist president, Klement Gottwald, and his successors became puppets of the Soviet regime, and during the 1950s the country suffered an era of Stalinist repression. Hundreds of people accused of anti-state activities were executed, while thousands more were locked up in prisons and concentration camps. Growing unrest in the 1960s exploded into student riots in 1966 and 1967, paving the way for a young Slovakian, Alexander Dubček, to take power from the old guard in the Prague Spring of 1968. Dubček's democratic reforms encouraged a brief flowering of freedom. But Czechoslovakia's Warsaw Pact neighbours saw his experiment as dangerous counter-revolution, and on 20 August, the 'flower' was crushed beneath the brutal Soviet tanks.

Dubček was exiled, and his successor, Gustáv Husák, set about overturning the democratic reforms and purging the Communist Party of hundreds of thousands of dissidents. Many educated professionals were kicked out of their jobs and forced to look for work as manual labourers. In 1977, a group of intellectuals signed a public petition called Charter 77, in which they criticized the Husák regime and made demands for democracy and human rights. Among the group, which soon became a focus for dissent, was Václav Havel, who paid for his pro-democratic activities with five years in prison. **21**

The Velvet Revolution

Havel was among those who were arrested in Prague's Wenceslas Square in January 1989, when police violently broke up demonstrations to mark the 20th anniversary of the death of Jan Palach, a student who had publicly burnt himself in protest against the Soviet occupation of 1968. In November 1989, popular unrest provoked by poor living standards and an oppressive regime, and encouraged by *perestroika* and the unravelling of the Iron Curtain, welled up in massive demonstrations in central Prague, climaxing in a rally of 750,000 people. Faced with overwhelming demands for reform, the Communist leaders resigned, and on 29 December 1989 Václav Havel, then leader of the opposition coalition called Civic Forum, was elected president. Because no blood had been shed, the overthrow was christened the Velvet Revolution.

The first free general election since 1946 produced a record-breaking 99% turnout, and a convincing majority for the Civic Forum. At once the new government set about a programme of restoring multi-party democracy and freedom of speech, returning property and businesses to private ownership, and moving towards a market-based economy. Growing tension between the Czech and Slovak administrations led in 1992 to an agreement to go their separate ways, and on New Year's Day in 1993, the state of Czechoslovakia ceased to exist. Following the Velvet Divorce, Prague became the administrative capital of the newly formed Czech Republic, composed of the ancient lands of Bohemia and Moravia.

The first years of freedom have been hard for the Czechs, as the country struggles to adapt to a new way of life, but things are steadily improving. Today, the Czech Republic has one of the fastest growing economies in eastern Europe, and is also one of its most popular tourist destinations. For the descendants of the princess and the ploughboy, the future is looking decidedly healthy.

Where to Go

Each of the various regions of the Czech Republic has its own particular character. West Bohemia, centred around the industrial, beer-brewing city of Plzeň, is a sparsely populated region of farmland and thickly wooded hills, famous for the spa towns of Karlovy Vary and Mariánské Lázně. The densely forested slopes of the Šumava mountains, along its south-western border with Germany, extend into South Bohemia, whose principal town, České Budějovice, is also known for its beer. This region has many noteworthy castles and monasteries situated along the banks of the Vltava, which rises in the Šumava hills and flows north towards Prague.

North and East Bohemia, though scarred by industry and pollution in some areas, boast some of the country's finest scenery in the 'rock towns' of Adršpach-Teplice and Český Ráj. To the east, the ancient kingdom of Moravia offers the fine old cities of Olomouc and Brno, and the pretty wooden architecture of Rožnov pod Radhoštěm. Across the border in neighbouring Slovakia, the capital Bratislava is an easy day's outing from Brno.

But first and most renowned is Prague, that 'symphony in stone', which is undoubtedly one of Europe's most romantic tourist destinations.

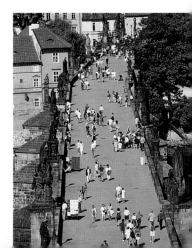

Tourists throng the parapet of Charles Bridge, Prague's most famous monument.

Czech Republic Highlights

Adršpach-Teplice Rocks. A scenic wonderland of thick pine forest and rugged hills, riven by deep valleys and soaring sandstone cliffs. A paradise for rock-climbers, and a popular playground for weekend walkers. Open dawn to dusk. Admission 25 Kč.

Český Krumlov. Bohemia's most beautiful town, watched over by a romantic Renaissance castle, has been placed on UNESCO's World Heritage List. Castle open 8am to 5pm May to August, from 9am April and September; closed Mondays, and October to March. Guided tour 70 Kč.

Hluboká Castle. The spectacular Neo-Gothic home of the Schwarzenberg family. Open 8am to 5pm June to August, from 9am May and September, and 9am to 4pm April and October; closed Mondays, and November to March. Guided tour 40 Kč.

Jindřichův Hradec. Historic seat of the Lords of Hradec, with one of the country's most interesting castles. Castle open 8am to 5pm May to August, from 9am April and September; closed Mondays, and October to March. Guided tour 25 Kč.

Karlovy Vary. The biggest, the oldest, and the most popular of Bohemia's spa towns, founded in 1358 by Charles IV. Attractions include hot mineral springs, forest walks, fine architecture, good restaurants, and a lively cultural scene.

Prague. The Czech capital is one of Europe's most beautiful and romantic cities, with a wealth of historical, architectural and cultural attractions. Castle buildings open 9am to 5pm; closed Mondays. Combined admission 80 Kč. Most museums and galleries are closed on Mondays.

Rožnov pod Radhoštěm. The town's Open-Air Museum contains examples of traditional wooden farmhouses, mills, churches and other buildings from villages throughout Wallachia. Open 9am to 6pm. Combined ticket for all three parts of museum, 40 Kč.

Vranov Castle. One of the country's finest examples of Baroque architecture. Open 9am to 6pm July and August, to 5pm May, June and September, and to 4pm (weekends only) April and October; closed Mondays, and November to March. Guided tour 35 Kč.

Prague (Praha)

Prague's reputation as one of Europe's most beautiful cities is justly deserved. Seen from the summit of Petřín Hill, its historic heart spreads beneath the castle in a colourful mosaic of red tile roofs, green domes and belfries, and delicate pink and ochre walls; its medieval skyline, pierced with Gothic pinnacles, has earned Prague the inspiring nickname, 'City of a Hundred Spires'.

Prague's principal sights are concentrated in the city centre, which is divided in two by a gentle sweep of the Vltava. Prague Castle and the Lesser Quarter lie on the west bank, linked by the medieval arches of Charles Bridge to the Old and New Towns on the east bank. If you have only one day to spend here, you can take in the city's highlights by following the Royal Way, the ancient, ceremonial route used by the Bohemian kings. It runs from the site of the old Royal Palace (near the Powder Tower) along Celetná and Karlova Streets, crosses Charles Bridge, then continues along Mostecká and Nerudova Streets as far as St Vitus Cathedral. This is where the coronation ceremony used to be performed. You can do the tour in this direction if you wish, but it is less strenuous to take a tram up to the castle and follow the route in reverse downhill all the way.

After a visit to the castle in the morning, walk down to the Lesser Quarter for something to eat. In the afternoon, cross Charles Bridge to explore the Old Town, and finish at the Powder Tower. In the evening you can take a stroll along Wenceslas Square, perhaps to enjoy a coffee in the splendid Hotel Europa. Remember that most museums and galleries (including the castle buildings) are closed on Mondays.

PRAGUE CASTLE (Pražský hrad)

A vast complex of ceremonial and administrative buildings, Prague Castle is encircled by massive walls extending along the crest of a ridge above the river. The castle, dominated by **25**

Follow the Signs

Here are some key words to help you around Prague:

hrad	castle
kaple	chapel
kostel	church
klášter	convent, monastery
město	town, city
most	bridge
muzeum	museum
nábřeží	embankment
náměstí	square
palác	palace
památník	monument
ulice	street
věž	tower
zahrada	garden

the soaring spires of St Vitus Cathedral, is more like a small town than a fortress, and is even recorded in the *Guinness Book of Records* as the world's largest medieval castle.

You can reach the castle by taking tram no. 22 from the Old Town embankment near Charles Bridge, which takes you to the northern gate. Or climb up through the Lesser Quarter as far as Hradčanské Square (*Hradčanské náměstí*) and the castle's main entrance gate, flanked by guards and sculptures of battling giants. Tourists gather here to watch the **changing of the guard** (every hour, on the hour, with a lengthier ceremony at noon).

Go past the sentries into the First Courtyard, then through the Baroque triumphal arch of the Matthias Gate and into the Second Courtyard. Ahead of you is the Chapel of the Holy Cross (*kaple sv. Kříže*), the old cathedral treasury, which now houses an information desk, currency exchange, toilets and ATM. To the left of the chapel another passage leads to the Third Courtyard, where you are immediately confronted by the massive west wall of **St Vitus Cathedral** (*katedrála sv. Víta*). Begun in 1344 on the orders of Charles IV, only the east end of the cathedral was completed by the early 15th century. Building work continued sporadically in the 16th and 17th centuries, but the cathedral was not finished until 1929 – almost 600 years after the foundations were laid! (Entrance to the nave is free, but you must pay to visit the choir, crypt and Wenceslas Chapel; one ticket allows admission to the cathedral, the Royal Palace, and St George's Basilica, and can be bought at any of these buildings.)

The soaring Gothic vault of the interior is lit by beautiful stained glass windows. In the ambulatory you will find the elaborate silver tomb of St John of Nepomuk, and by the south porch the **Wenceslas Chapel**, where the tomb of St Wenceslas is surrounded by fabulous 14th-century frescoes and walls inset with polished precious stones. Nearby is the entrance to the **Royal Crypt**, which contains the tombs of famed Czech rulers (including

Prague's vast castle complex dominates the city from its commanding hilltop position.

Charles IV, Wenceslas IV and Emperor Ferdinand I), and the foundations of the 10th- and 11th-century churches which preceded the cathedral. If you are feeling energetic, you can climb up a seemingly endless spiral staircase to the top of the **Bell Tower** for a magnificent view over the city.

Leave the cathedral and go left into the Third Courtyard, where you can marvel at the building's impressive southern facade. The intricate Gothic arches and ribbed vaults of the south porch (known as the Golden Portal) are the masterpiece of architect Peter Parler. Unfortunately, his Gothic Bell Tower was left unfinished, and it was capped with a bulging Baroque spire in the 16th century. Beneath the tower is a bronze statue of St George and the Dragon (a copy – the 14th-century original is in the National Gallery), and a granite obelisk commemorating those who died in World War I.

The **Old Royal Palace** (*Starý Královský palác*), just across the courtyard, is the secular equivalent of the huge

cathedral. It was home to the kings of Bohemia until the 16th century, when the Habsburgs turned it into offices and warehouses. Its centrepiece is the splendid **Vladislav Hall** (*Vladislavský sál*), which has a beautiful late-Gothic vaulted ceiling (1493-1502), with elegant, curving ribs interlocking in leaf and petal designs. It is known as the largest secular hall of the Middle Ages built without the support of dome or pillars. Off one end is a series of small chambers, known as the **Bohemian Chancellery**, where the famous Defenestration of Prague took place in 1618 (see p.17). At the other end of the Vladislav Hall is the **Hall of the Diet**, where the supreme court used to sit, and next to it is the astonishing **Riders' Staircase**. More a ramp than a stair, this narrow passage was used by mounted knights to gain access to the Vladislav Hall, the venue for indoor jousting tournaments during the 16th century.

The Riders' Staircase exits into St George's Square, overlooked by the **Basilica of St**

George (*bazilika sv. Jiří*), whose Baroque facade conceals a beautiful Romanesque church, founded in 905. The neighbouring **Convent of St George** houses the National Gallery's collection of old Bohemian art from the Gothic, Renaissance and Baroque periods. The narrow street to the right of the basilica leads to the castle's east gate, where you can double back along a terrace garden and return to Hradčanské Square. A passage off the north side of the square leads to the **Sternberg Palace** (*Šternberský palác*), one of Prague's best picture galleries,

The Gothic vaults of Vladislav Hall once echoed to the sounds of jousting tournaments.

which houses a collection of European art from the 14th to the 19th centuries.

Two more attractions lie a short walk west of the square. The **Loretto** (*Loreta*) is a grandiose Baroque sanctuary at whose heart lies the *Santa Casa* (Holy House), a replica of the House of the Virgin Mary in Loreto, Italy. The Italian house is supposed to have **29**

The Strahov Monastery library ceiling (above); Church of St Nicholas, Lesser Quarter (right).

whose sumptuous interior is adorned with gilded stucco and painted ceilings. From here you can walk around the cloisters to the **Treasury**, a small but glittering collection of precious reliquaries, monstrances and chalices made of gold and silver, and studded with hundreds of diamonds.

Beyond the Loreto, on the edge of Petřín Hill, the complex of **Strahov Monastery** (*Strahovský klášter*) is situated amidst tall trees. Founded in 1140, the present buildings date from the 17th and 18th centuries. Much is closed to the public, but you can visit the library and peer into the magnificent Theological and Philosophical Halls. The former was built in the 1670s, the latter in the 1780s and 1790s; both are decorated with superb painted ceilings. The libraries are connected by a corridor that has displays of curiosities, including a collection of horticultural books – each volume is devoted to a single species of tree, with the covers made from the tree's wood, and the spine decorated with its bark.

been miraculously transported there by angels, and the replica in Prague was built in 1626 as part of a Counter-Reformation attempt to re-Catholicize Bohemia. The cloisters were built in the late 17th century, and the Baroque facade added in the 1740s. The *Santa Casa* is decorated with stucco depictions of Old Testament figures and scenes from the life of the Virgin Mary. Behind it is the

30 larger **Church of the Nativity**,

LESSER QUARTER
(Malá Strana)

The district between the castle and the river is known as the Lesser Quarter. Founded in the 13th century but subsequently destroyed by fire, it owes its present charm to the Baroque rebuilding of the 17th and 18th centuries. At its heart, **Lesser Quarter Square** (*Malostranské náměstí*) is a pleasingly arcaded plaza that is lined with tourist restaurants. The square is divided into two parts by the huge green dome and bell-tower of the **Church of St Nicholas** (*kostel sv. Mikuláše*), one of Europe's most majestic Baroque buildings, begun in 1703 by the famous father-and-son team of Christoph and Kilian Ignaz Dientzenhofer and completed in 1755. The interior is almost overwhelming, with its lavish confection of gilded stucco, trompe-l'œil painting, simulated marble and brightly frescoed ceilings, and adorned with golden cherubim and seraphim, sternly watched over by four towering statues of the church fathers.

Off the northeast corner of the square, Letenská Street leads off to the entrance to the **Wallenstein Garden** (*Valdštejnská zahrada*), a lovely landscaped garden overlooked by the Renaissance facade of the Wallenstein Palace. Both were created for the powerful General Albrecht von Wallenstein in the early 17th century. From the square's southeast corner, Mostecká Street leads to the leafy lanes of Kampa Island, and to Prague's most famous monument.

Architecture through the Ages

The Czech Republic contains a wealth of outstanding architecture, with many fine examples of building styles from different periods. Here is a brief review of the main styles referred to in the text, with suggestions of buildings that exemplify each one.

Romanesque (11th-12th centuries). The style originated in the monasteries of 10th- and 11th-century Europe, and is characterized by semi-circular Roman arches on doors and windows, semi-circular barrel-vaulted roofs, and massive piers and walls with few windows (interior of St George's Basilica in Prague Castle; Přemysl Palace, Olomouc).

Gothic (12th-15th centuries). Evolved from Romanesque, as stone masons attempted to build higher and wider vaults; characterized by high, ribbed vaults, pointed arches, and tall, thin windows with elaborate tracery (St Vitus Cathedral, Prague; Cathedral of St Barbara, Kutná Hora). Elements of the Gothic style were revived in the 19th century as Neo-Gothic (country house at Lednice).

Renaissance (15th-17th centuries). Arose out of a rediscovery of the classical architecture of ancient Greece and Rome; it is characterized by classical facades, arcades, dormer windows, elaborate stepped gables, and sgraffito decoration (Wallenstein Palace, Prague; Telč Castle, Moravia).

Baroque (17th-18th centuries). Developed hand-in-hand with the Catholic Counter-Reformation; characterized by monumental grandeur, exuberant decoration, rich colours, curved surfaces, oval shapes, trompe-l'œil paintings and frescoed ceilings (Church of St Nicholas in Prague's Lesser Quarter; Vranov Castle, Moravia).

Art Nouveau (c.1890-1910). A decorative style that flourished briefly at the turn of the century; characterized by graceful, sinuous lines, usually based on trees, flowers and leaves, and painted or sculpted decoration, often of flowers and female figures (Municipal House and Grand Hotel Europa, Prague). The most famous Czech exponent of the style was Alfons Mucha (1860-1939).

Cubist (early 20th century). Inspired by Picasso, shadows on angular surfaces create form (House of the Black Madonna, Prague).

The 16 arches of **Charles Bridge** (*Karlův most*) were built in the late 14th century on the orders of Charles IV, and, despite occasional flood damage, have survived intact to the present day. The bridge is closed to traffic, and now serves as an open-air gallery-cum-stage for the scores of artists, musicians, jugglers and other buskers who entertain the tourist crowds. The parapet is adorned with a series of 30 statues and sculptural groups, which date from the 17th-20th centuries (though copies are gradually replacing the worn originals). The oldest and most famous is the 1683 statue of St John Nepomuk (about halfway across on the downstream side), crowned with a halo of five stars. Jan Nepomucký was thrown into the river in 1393 after a disagreement with the king, and was later hailed as a Catholic martyr during the Counter-Reformation. Below the statue is a bronze relief that depicts the scene. The figure of the saint has been polished by the fingers of passers-by, who touch it for good luck.

OLD TOWN
(Staré Město)

The east end of Charles Bridge is dominated by the distinctive wedge spire of the **Old Town Bridge Tower**, whose parapet provides one of the best viewpoints over the city. The late 14th-century Gothic tower is decorated on the landward side with a statue of St Vitus, who is flanked by kings Charles IV (to the left) and Wenceslas IV.

Pass beneath the tower and join the crowds that throng narrow Karlova Street, which leads to **Old Town Square** (*Staroměstské náměstí*), the heart of medieval Prague. The huge square was originally a market-place in the 11th century, and since that time it has witnessed many of the city's most historically momentous events. It was here that 27 Protestant martyrs were put to death in 1621, and here, too, that Klement Gottwald proclaimed the Socialist Republic of Czechoslovakia in 1948. Just 20 years later Soviet tanks rumbled across the cobblestones and put paid to the first **33**

Virgin and Child gaze down from the Gothic gable of Our Lady before Týn.

Church of Our Lady before Týn (*kostel Panny Marie před Týnem*). Dating from the 14th century, this Gothic fantasy was once the city's leading Hussite church, but the gold chalice (symbol of the Hussites) that adorned the gable was melted down to make a halo for the statue of the Virgin Mary that replaced it following the Catholic victory at the Battle of the White Mountain (see p.17). The rather gloomy interior is notable only for the tomb of Tycho Brahe (1546-1601), the talented astronomer.

Opposite the church is the less extravagant tower of the **Old Town Hall** (*Staroměstská radnice*), which dates from the 14th century. The top of the tower provides a grand view of the square, but the main attraction is at its foot. Here you will find the famous **Astronomical Clock**, whose complex dials-within-dials display not only the time, but also the phases of the moon and the position of the sun relative to the signs of the zodiac. Beneath the clock is a calendar disk, with twelve circular paintings representing

flowerings of the democracy movement. Today, history has given way to hedonism, and the square provides a dramatic backdrop to a colourful bustle of tourists, shoppers, buskers and open-air cafés.

Three important buildings dominate the square. As you approach from Charles Bridge you cannot fail to miss the twin, pinnacled spires of the

the months of the year, and divided around the rim into 365 days, each marked with the saint whose feast is celebrated on that day. Crowds gather to see the clock strike the hour, when the figure of Death to the right of the dial tolls a bell, and effigies of the 12 apostles led by St Peter parade past the windows above.

The wedding-cake facade of the **Church of St Nicholas** (*kostel sv. Mikuláše*) stands in stark contrast to the Gothic severity of Týn Church and the Town Hall. Built in 1732-35 by Kilian Ignaz Dientzenhofer (who also had a major hand in the church of St Nicholas in the Lesser Quarter, see p.31), its imposing interior is capped by a magnificent frescoed cupola, and a vast crown-shaped chandelier is suspended above the nave. Ironically, while the once-Hussite Týn is now a Catholic church, this monument to the Catholic Counter-Reformation was granted in 1920 to the Czechoslovak Hussite Church. The square has other reminders of the Hussite movement – beneath

St Nicholas stands Ladislav Šaloun's bronze **Monument to Jan Hus**, unveiled in 1915; and in the paving below the Town Hall tower are 27 white crosses, commemorating the 27 Protestant martyrs who were executed here in 1621.

Picturesque Celetná Street, one of the city's most ancient thoroughfares, leads eastward from the square to the **Powder Tower** (*Prašná brána*), a huge Gothic gate-tower built in the late 15th century and modelled on Old Town Bridge Tower. It was originally flanked by a Royal Palace, but following riots in 1483 the king moved his court to the safety of the castle. The abandoned palace was demolished in the early 1900s and replaced with the magnificent **Municipal House** (*Obecní dům*), perhaps the country's foremost example of Art Nouveau architecture. Designed as a cultural complex of exhibition rooms and concert halls, its centrepiece is the glass-domed Smetana Hall, decorated with allegorical wall paintings and sculptures by leading Czech artists.

35

JOSEFOV

From the northern edge of Old Town Square, the grand boulevard of Pařížská Street cuts an Art Nouveau swathe through one of Prague's oldest districts. This area was once the city's Jewish Quarter, named Josefov after the enlightened Emperor Josef II, who relaxed many of the draconian laws that once discriminated against the Jewish community. At its height, Josefov was home to over 50,000 Jews, but slum clearances at the turn of the 20th century followed by the Holocaust of World War II all but annihilated the population. Today, there are only about 1,000 Jews living in Prague.

The few remnants of old Josefov that have survived are protected under the aegis of the **State Jewish Museum** (*Státní židovské muzeum*). One ticket gives access to six historic sites. The Neo-Gothic **Maisel Synagogue** (*Maiselova synagóga*) is named after a 16th-century mayor of the ghetto, and houses an exhibition of liturgical silver. The **Pinkas Synagogue** (*Pinkasova synagóga*), just around the corner in Široká Street, is a moving memorial to the Holocaust – the names of all the 77,297 Czech Jews who were murdered by the Nazis are inscribed on the interior walls.

From the Pinkas Synagogue a gate gives access to the **Old**

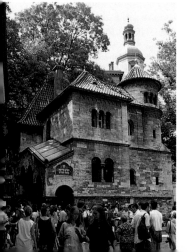

The narrow streets of Josefov were once stalked by the Golem, a mythical monster.

Rabbi Löw

Jehuda Löw ben Bezalel, better known as Rabbi Löw, was a Chief Rabbi of Prague in the 16th century. An accomplished scholar and theologian, he also dabbled in alchemy and astrology, and studied the mystical writings of the cabbala. He was thought to have magical powers, which he used to create an artificial being called the Golem, made from clay. Rabbi Löw brought the creature to life by placing a magic word in its mouth, but when it ran amok he removed the word, and hid the Golem in the clay beneath the Old-New Synagogue.

Jewish Cemetery (*Židovský hřbitov*), where over 12,000 tombstones crowd together in the sun-dappled shade of a stand of elder trees. The last burial to take place here was in 1787, when a new cemetery (where author Franz Kafka is buried) was opened in the suburb of Žižkov. The crush of headstones remains a powerful symbol of the overcrowding in the ghetto. The most famous tomb, that of Rabbi Löw, is marked by dozens of tightly folded scraps of paper bearing scribbled prayers, wedged in cracks in the stone or held in place by pebbles.

At the far end of the cemetery is the **Ceremonial Hall** (*Obřadní síň*), built in Neo-Romanesque style in the 19th century. It houses a poignant exhibition of drawings made by children deported to the Terezín concentration camp (see p.83). Next door is the **Klaus Synagogue** (*Klausova synagóga*), with an exhibition that illustrates the works of Jewish scholars, artists and scientists, including those of the famous Rabbi Löw.

East of the cemetery, the most fascinating building in the Jewish quarter is the **Old-New Synagogue** (*Staronová synagóga*), tucked beneath the Baroque clock tower of the Jewish Town Hall. It is known as Europe's oldest surviving **37** synagogue, dating from the middle of the 13th century. Its unusual stepped brick gables conceal a Gothic vaulted hall whose floor is at least 1.5m (5ft) below the present street level. In the centre a beautiful 15th-century iron grille surrounds the cantor's platform. There's also a faded banner bearing the Star of David, presented by Emperor Ferdinand II in 1648 in recognition of the Jews' support during the war against the Swedes.

NEW TOWN (Nové Město)

Despite its name, Prague's New Town has a pretty ancient pedigree – it was founded by Charles IV in 1348 to relieve overcrowding in the adjoining Old Town. A programme of slum clearance in the 19th century destroyed all the medieval buildings, and today's New Town dates mostly from the late 19th and 20th centuries.

The focal point of the New Town is the broad boulevard known as **Wenceslas Square** (*Václavské náměstí*), which sweeps 700m (765yds) from the edge of the Old Town up to the monumental facade of the **National Museum** (*Národní muzeum*). The museum is visited more for its architecture and its grand view of the boulevard than for its rather dull and academic collections of historical objects. The view is dominated by an equestrian statue of the Czechs' patron saint, St Wenceslas, which was erected in 1912. It was near this spot that another national hero, the student Jan Palach, burnt himself alive in 1969 in a protest against Soviet oppression. Today the square is a thriving monument to capitalism, lined with shops, hotels, supermarkets, travel agents, discos, clubs and restaurants.

From the Old Town end of Wenceslas Square, Národní třída leads west to the Vltava, where the **National Theatre** (*Národní divadlo*) dominates the riverbank. This grand Neo-Renaissance structure, built in 1868-83, was restored in the 1980s; its striking blue and gold roof covered with stars is a familiar city landmark.

Museum and Gallery Highlights

Before you plan your visit, it's wise to check precise opening times at the tourist information office.

Antonín Dvořák Museum (*Muzeum A. Dvořáka*): Ke Karlovu 20, Prague 2; 10am-5pm daily except Monday; Metro C: I. P. Pavlova. Memorable music in fabulous Baroque villa devoted to the life and works of the Czech composer.

Bertramka: Mozartova 169, Prague 5; 9.30am-6pm daily, indoor concerts at 5pm Thursday, Friday and Saturday; trams 4, 6, 7, 9. Mozartian memorabilia in a delightful setting.

Collection of Old Bohemian Art (*Sbírka starého českého umění*): St George's Convent, Jiřské náměstí 33, Prague Castle; 10am-6pm Tuesday to Sunday, closed Monday; Metro A: Hradčanská; tram 22 to Pražský hrad. The National Gallery's treasured Baroque paintings in a 1000-year-old former convent.

Museum of Decorative Arts (*Uměleckoprůmyslové muzeum*): 17 Listopadu 2, Prague 1; 10am-6pm daily except Monday; trams 17, 18. Displays of Czech crystal and porcelain.

National Gallery European Collection (*Veletržní Palác/Národní galerie*): Dukelských hrdinů 47; 10am-6pm daily except Monday; trams 5, 12, 17 Veletržní stop. 19th & 20th century European art. (See also p.29 Šternberský Palác).

National Technical Museum (*Národní technické muzeum*): Kostelní 42, Prague 7; 9am-5pm daily except Monday; walk up Kostelní towards the Letná Plain. Fascinating collection of old planes, trains and other technological achievements.

St Agnes' Convent (*Klášter sv. Anežky*): Anežská, on the corner of U milosrdných; 10am-6pm daily except Monday; trams 5, 14, 26; bus 125. The National Gallery's collection of 19th-century Czech painting in a restored wing of a Gothic convent.

State Jewish Museum (*Státní židovské muzeum*): Jáchymova 3, Prague 1; 9am-5pm (last entry 4.30pm) daily except Saturdays and Jewish holidays; Metro A: Staroměstská. Exhibits documenting Prague's Jewish community in historic synagogues.

Excursions from Prague

There are many fascinating sights that can easily be visited on a day-trip from Prague. Trips can be arranged at any travel agent (see Guides and Tours, p.126). The following are a few suggestions.

KARLŠTEJN

Karlštejn Castle, which lies about 32km (20 miles) south-west of Prague, was founded by Emperor Charles IV in the 14th century as a stronghold for the crown jewels and holy relics. Restored in the 19th century, it is now the Czech Republic's most visited castle outside of Prague. Seen from the village below, its Gothic towers and crenellated walls embody everyone's idea of the perfect Bohemian castle. Inside, however, the castle is a little disappointing. The Royal Apartments are gloomy and bare, and the only remnant of their original decor is some 14th-century wood-panelling in the throne room.

The **Chapel of Our Lady** is more interesting, with its 14th-century murals depicting the Apocalypse, scenes from the castle's history, and the image of Charles IV himself kneeling before a cross. A door in the corner of the chapel led to the emperor's own private **Chapel of St Catherine**, where he would lock himself up and meditate for hours or even days at a time; a small hole in the wall allowed servants to pass through food and drink, and important documents that required Charles's signature.

The highlight of the castle is the Gothic **Chapel of the Holy Rood**, which is situated in the Great Tower. It was here, in a safe behind the altar, that the crown jewels were kept. The chapel is famed for its remarkable decoration – the walls are decorated with painted panels of the saints, and encrusted with thousands of precious and semi-precious stones, while the gilded ceiling is inset with hundreds of glass stars, a silver disc representing the moon, and a golden one for the sun. (The Chapel of the Holy Rood

*K*řivoklát Castle was once a favourite hunting retreat of King Wenceslas IV.

has been closed for restoration since 1980; although it was due to re-open in 1996, you should check with the tourist office before arranging a visit.)

KŘIVOKLÁT

The pointed tower of Křivoklát Castle rises like a lighthouse above a vast rolling ocean of trees, about 40km (25 miles) west of Prague. The forest was a traditional hunting ground of the Bohemian kings, and the castle, founded in 1109, was a favourite retreat of Wenceslas IV, an obsessive huntsman. It later came into the possession of the powerful Wallenstein family, before being sold to the Fürstenbergs in 1685. The guided tour includes the stunning late-Gothic **chapel**, with its elaborately carved wooden stalls from the 15th century; the impressive **King's Hall**,

with its elegant vaulting; and the Fürstenbergs' **library**. The early-Gothic basement that is beneath the chapel was once used as a **prison**, and contains a display of grisly medieval torture instruments.

KONOPIŠTĚ

Situated not far from the town of Benešov, about 44km (27 miles) south of Prague, is the stately castle of Konopiště. The tall, machicolated round towers betray the castle's medieval origins, but most of the building dates from the late 19th century when it was rebuilt in Neo-Gothic style. Its **41**

*O*ver 300,000 hunting trophies decorate the walls of Neo-Gothic Konopiště Castle.

then owner was the Archduke Franz Ferdinand, whose assassination by Gavrilo Princip in 1914 marked the start of World War I. The archduke had a passion for hunting that verged on mania – an estimated 300,000 hunting trophies adorn the castle walls, from birds, badgers and polecats, through wild boar and deer, to bears, tigers **42** and antelope, each one marked

scrupulously with the date and place it was killed.

There are three guided tours to choose from. One tour takes you through the apartments on the first floor of the south wing, which are flanked by a long corridor crammed with thousands of hunting trophies. Gorgeously furnished with 17th-century Italian cabinets and Meissen porcelain, the apartments include the **Great Dining Room**, with its finely woven tapestries, and a ceiling painted with figures representing Morning, Noon, Evening and Night; the **bedchambers** used by Kaiser Wilhelm II and Admiral Alfred von Tirpitz on their visit in June 1914; and an original **bathroom** complete with fixtures and fittings from 1900. The other tours take in the private apartments of the Archduke Franz Ferdinand and his family, the armoury, the chapel, and an exhibition on the history of the castle. There is also a gallery devoted to paintings, drawings and sculptures of St George, who was another of the archduke's curious obsessions.

KUTNÁ HORA

The former silver-mining town of Kutná Hora, situated about 65km (40 miles) to the east of Prague, offers one of the most varied and interesting day-trips from the capital. Plentiful silver deposits were found in the surrounding hills in the late 12th century, and Wenceslas II (1278-1305) soon founded the Royal Mint here. For several hundred years Kutná Hora was the second most important city in Bohemia after Prague, but quickly went into decline in the mid-16th century when the silver ran out. Today the town wears an air of faded grandeur.

The town's most impressive monument is the magnificent **St Barbara's Cathedral** (*kostel sv. Barbory*), founded in 1388 but left unfinished in the 1550s; the west facade was not built until 1894-1910. It is one of the finest Gothic churches in Europe, flanked by graceful flying buttresses and topped by an astonishing three-peaked, tented roof. Enter the church on the north side. To your left is the altar, with an ambulatory around it bordered by eight small chapels. The three that are furthest from the entrance contain some interesting 15th-century frescoes, including scenes of miners at work. The central one of the three, known as the **Smíšek Chapel**, has the Crucifixion on the left wall, and the Queen of Sheba and Solomon on the right; the back wall shows the eponymous Smíšek (a rich mine-owner) with his sons, while angels and miners decorate the vault.

A terrace road leads north from the cathedral to the **Hrádek**, meaning Little Castle. A Gothic building that once formed part of the city walls, today it houses the **Mining Museum**, which offers tours through a section of medieval mine shaft.

The town's other attraction is the **Italian Court** (*Vlašský Dvůr*), beyond the Hrádek and just south of the main square. The court originally served as the Royal Mint, and it was also used as a royal residence by Wenceslas IV (1378-1419). When the mines closed, it was turned into the Town Hall. The **43**

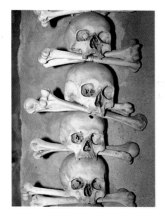

*S*edlec Ossuary offers the grisly spectacle of decorations fashioned from human bones.

15th-century **Audience Hall**, still with its original coffered, wooden ceiling, contains two 19th-century murals depicting important events which took place within its walls – the election of Vladislav Jagellonský as king (1471), and a meeting between Wenceslas IV and Jan Hus (1409). The **44** tiny chapel of St Wenceslas,

founded by Wenceslas IV, was redecorated at the turn of the 20th century in Art Nouveau style.

On the edge of town, in the grounds of Sedlec Monastery, an altogether more ghoulish spectacle awaits. The **Sedlec Ossuary** (*kostnice Sedlec*) contains the bones of more than 30,000 people, many of whom died in a great plague in the 14th century. Others were also keen to be buried here, since it was believed that a 13th-century abbot had sanctified the graveyard with soil brought from Golgotha. The Schwarzenberg family bought the monastery in the late 18th century, and in 1870 they commissioned a local woodcarver called František Rinta to 'do something artistic' with the bones. The fruits of his labour can be seen in the underground chapel – four huge bell-shaped mounds of bones, a chandelier using every bone in the human body, and the Schwarzenberg coat of arms in bones. Rinta even signed his name in bones – look on the right-hand side of the steps as you enter.

West Bohemia

The western part of the Czech Republic consists of a sparsely populated region of forests and hills, popular with Czech and German hikers and weekend campers. The main attractions are the three historic spa towns of Karlovy Vary, Mariánské Lázně and Františkovy Lázně, and the world-famous Pilsner Urquell Brewery in Plzeň.

PLZEŇ

The regional capital of West Bohemia is Plzeň, known to the Germans as Pilsen, and famed throughout the world as the birthplace of the hoppy lager beer known as Pilsner, which has been brewed here since the Middle Ages. Plzeň's other claim to fame is the Škoda Engineering Works, founded by Emil Škoda in the 19th century, and still manufacturing heavy machinery, railway locomotives, trucks and cars. Plzeň is a modern industrial city with a population of 175,000 people, but the medieval town centre still has a few interesting sights.

The focus of the old town is **Republic Square** (*náměstí Republiky*), an enormous plaza lined with grimy buildings and dominated by the huge bulk of **St Bartholomew's Cathedral** (*kostel sv. Bartoloměje*). This

*C*limb the 298 steps to the top of St Bartholomew's steeple – Bohemia's tallest.

The interior of the church at Kladruby is a graceful blend of Gothic and Baroque elements.

austere Gothic church was constructed between the 14th and 16th centuries, and boasts the tallest steeple in Bohemia (103m/338 ft).

Beside the church is a 1681 Plague Column, and beyond it the 16th-century Renaissance Town Hall. If you go right here along Pražská Street, then left on Perlová, you will find the entrance to the **Underground Passages**. Here you can join a 30-minute tour through a labyrinth of tunnels and cellars that were burrowed into the rock beneath the old town in medieval times. The passages

and chambers were used for brewing and storing beer (the temperature is maintained at a constant of 10sC/50sF), and as hiding places in less settled times. Each cellar had its own private well, and some even had their own drinking dens. At the far end of Perlová Street is a worthy **Brewery Museum** (*Pivovarské muzeum*).

The most popular attraction is undoubtedly the **Pilsner Urquell Brewery** (*Plzeňský prazdroj pivovar*). Beer was originally brewed in the cellars of the old town, but in the 19th century the individual brewers decided to pool their resources and erect a municipal brewery that would exploit the newest technology to reap the benefits of scale. The resulting beer, Pilsner Urquell (which means the 'Fountainhead of Pilsner beer'), has been brewed on this site since 1842; the label that adorns the bottle has an image of the double-arched gate at the entrance. Guided tours are conducted daily Monday to Saturday at 12.30pm, finishing off with a tasting session, then lunch in the brewery's own beer-hall. Tours can be booked through ČEDOK (see Tourist Information Offices on p.135). An annual beer festival is held in October.

KLADRUBY

The Benedictine Monastery of Kladruby lies about 35km (22 miles) west of Plzeň, not far from the town of Stříbro. The monastery was founded by Prince Vladislav I in 1115, and by the 14th century it had become the richest in Bohemia. It was badly damaged during the Hussite campaigns and the Thirty Years' War, but it was able to regain its importance during the latter half of the 17th century. The monastery church, rebuilt in 1712-26 by Giovanni Santini, is one of the most harmonious examples of Gothic-Baroque architecture in Europe.

The church has undergone recent restoration, but the rest of the monastery buildings are in poor repair. The tour takes you into the Winter Refectory, with its marble floor and rich stucco decoration, and then to a display of Baroque sculpture in the cloister. But the real highlight is Santini's splendid **Church of the Holy Virgin**. The lofty interior, painted a pale, duck-egg green, is a skilful blend of Gothic form – tall, narrow nave with lancet windows in the apse and intricate ribbed vaults – with exuberant Baroque ornamentation. The ornate wooden altar, painted to look like red-brown marble, is also a mixture of Gothic and Baroque devices. A statue of the Virgin Mary, surrounded by a gilded halo, is flanked by the figures of the monastery's patron saints, Benedict and Wolfgang. Beneath her feet is a tiny and unique statue of the Crucifixion – Christ is nailed to the Cross by His left hand only; His right hand cups the wound in His side, from which the Sacred Blood spouts forth, to be collected in the Holy **47**

Grail. The pulpit is also worth admiring. Carved from pear and walnut wood, it takes the shape of a ship's prow (the image of the Catholic Church as a ship tossed on stormy seas was a popular one), and has an unusual pentagonal canopy.

 ## KARLOVY VARY (Karlsbad)

The far western corner of Bohemia is famous for its hot springs. For hundreds of years these mineralized waters have been used in the treatment of all kinds of illnesses, ranging from skin disorders to digestive complaints. From the 17th century onwards, the spas of Bohemia became increasingly fashionable as health resorts for the European aristocracy, who flocked here during the 'season' not only to 'take the cure', but to enjoy the many concerts and parties that were an integral part of the resorts' appeal. Music was an important feature of spa society, and over the years many famous composers visited, including Bach, Beethoven, Brahms and

Dvořák. Although the heyday of the spa towns was back in the 18th and 19th centuries, 'the cure' is still popular with visitors today, and many hotels continue to offer programmes of treatment involving mineral baths, mud packs, and 'taking the waters'.

The biggest, oldest, and most popular of Bohemia's spa towns is Karlovy Vary (Karlsbad in German), founded in 1358 by Charles IV, who is said to have happened upon the original spring while out hunting. The old town is set picturesquely in the wooded valley of the River Teplá, some distance away from the urban sprawl of the modern Karlovy Vary. Leave your vehicle in one of the many car parks and explore on foot.

Twin promenades run along the banks of the Teplá, lined with hotels, restaurants and shops, and passing all the main spas. Beginning at the downstream end, nearest the new town, you cannot fail to see the immense concrete bulk of the Thermal Hotel, purpose-built in the Communist era in order to provide spa holidays for tired workers. In the pretty, flower-bedecked Dvořák Park across the river is the wrought-iron **Park Colonnade** (*Sadová kolonáda*), dating from 1880-81, the first of five colonnades containing fountains that dispense the hot spring waters. Visitors who are here to take the cure walk from spring to spring, sipping the mineralized waters from special porcelain mugs with a spout in the handle, and nibbling sweet wafers called *oplatky* to take away the rather unsavoury taste.

Next is the **Mill Colonnade** (*Mlýnská kolonáda*), a grand Neo-Classical structure that was built in 1871-81 by Josef Zítek, the same architect that designed Prague's National Theatre. Statues depicting the 12 months of the year adorn its facade. Beyond, at the point where the river bends to the right, is the wooden **Market**

*B*rightly painted buildings line the banks of the River Teplá in Karlovy Vary.

49

Visitors sampling the hot spring waters at Karlovy Vary's Sprudel Colonnade.

50 — **Colonnade** (*Tržní kolonáda*), which dates from 1883, and houses the Charles IV spring. A relief above the fountain depicts the legend of the spring's discovery. Across the street, and spanning the river, is the modern **Sprudel Colonnade** (*Vřídelní kolonáda*), a rather ugly construction that houses the most famous of the town's

springs. The Sprudel (*Vřidlo*) is a mini-geyser that spouts very hot water ($72°C/160°F$) at up to 2000 litres (440 gallons) a minute. A glass dome encloses the head of the fountain, which gasps and wheezes and spurts jets of hot water up to 10m (33ft) in the air. Gentler fountains in the neighbouring hall allow cure-takers to try the waters. On the hillside above the colonnade is the beautiful Baroque church of **St Mary Magdalene** (*kostel sv. Máří Magdalény*), built in 1732-36 by Kilian Ignaz Dientzenhofer, who is best known for his masterpiece in Prague, the Church of St Nicholas in the Lesser Quarter (see p.31).

Beyond the Sprudel, carry on along the right bank (facing upstream). This stretch, known as the **Stará Louka**, is the town's prime shopping street, and includes the renowned Moser crystal shop and the stylish Café Elefant. At the end, where the river bends to the left, is the huge wedding-cake facade of the Grand Hotel Pupp, established in 1793 and still the best hotel in town. The present Neo-Baroque pile was put up in the late 19th century, and includes a splendid rococo dining room, a large, ornate concert hall, and a casino.

Down an alley, at the right-hand side of the hotel, is the lower station of a funicular railway that will take you to a hilltop viewpoint known as **Diana**. Here there is a wooden viewing tower which affords a superb panorama of wooded hills, with the red-tiled roofs of Karlovy Vary nestling in the valley below. This is also the starting point for a number of forest walks, one of which is a pleasant and leisurely stroll back down the hill to the town.

In addition to architectural and balneological attractions, Karlovy Vary plays host to a wide range of cultural events, including classical concerts, art exhibitions, and an annual International Film Festival in July. Free concerts are held at the Mill Colonnade at 4.30pm, Wednesday to Friday.

LOKET

The picturesque town of Loket is situated in a loop of the River Ohre, 12km (7 miles) southwest of Karlovy Vary. The main square, which is lined with medieval buildings, sits beneath the 14th-century

The Thirteenth Spring

A local physician called Dr David Becher was the first man to make a scientific study of the hot springs of Karlovy Vary (in 1789). It was he who invented the unusual porcelain mugs called becher cups, with a spout in the handle through which you can suck the water. His best-known invention, however, is the alcoholic herbal liqueur called *Becherovka*, a sticky, dark-brown concoction that tastes like cough medicine. It is jokingly called the 13th spring, and cynics claim that it is the only one that truly succeeds in making you feel better!

Gothic castle, perched spectacularly atop a cliff above the river. A steep lane and some steps lead up to the castle, which contains a Romanesque chapel and a small exhibition of local ceramics.

CHEB

The frontier outpost of Cheb lies 40km (25 miles) southwest of Karlovy Vary, and only 8km (5 miles) from the German border. It has changed hands many times through its history, and it suffered greatly during the Thirty Years' War. The town recovered in the 19th century, but was almost wholly depopulated when its German inhabitants were expelled after World War II.

At the centre of Cheb is the sloping triangle of **George of Poděbrady Square** (*náměstí krále Jiřího z Poděbrad*), lined with attractive old buildings. Prominent at the foot of the square is a block of rickety, half-timbered town houses that date from the 16th century, known as the **Špalíček** (Little Block), with the local museum behind it. Part of the museum building is the house in which Albrecht von Wallenstein, the famous, immensely wealthy and powerful military commander of the Habsburg army during the Thirty Years' War, was assassinated in 1634.

The chapel in Cheb Castle contains some very beautiful early Gothic vaulting.

To the northwest of the square, the **castle** was founded by Frederick Barbarossa in 1167 as an eastern outpost of the Holy Roman Empire. Red-brick fortifications, built in the 17th century, surround the forbidding Black Tower and a well-restored late 12th-century chapel in transitional style, with Romanesque doors, windows and column capitals, and Gothic ribbed cross-vaults.

FRANTIŠKOVY LÁZNĚ (Franzenbad)

A few miles north of Cheb lies Františkovy Lázně, the smallest and least visited of West Bohemia's three principal spa towns. It was founded in 1793, and named after the Habsburg Emperor Franz II. Blocks of elegant 19th-century Neo-Classical buildings, all painted a deep yellow with dazzlingly white stucco trim, stand at the centre of a large, landscaped park. The town's main source of mineral water is the Francis Spring (*Františkův pramen*), at the foot of the main street in an Empire-style pavilion built in 1831. A brisk 20-minute walk through the wooded park beyond the spring brings you to an attractive boating pond.

MARIÁNSKÉ LÁZNĚ (Marienbad)

The youngest West Bohemian spa town, Mariánské Lázně was founded by a local abbot in 1809. During the following decades an elegant resort grew up in an attractive landscaped park amid pine-covered hills, soon rivalling Karlovy Vary in popularity. A favourite retreat of the British monarch Edward VII, the town drew many other celebrities, including writers Mark Twain and Franz Kafka, the poet Goethe, and composers Wagner and Chopin.

There are about 40 springs, all cool and carbonated. The original gusher, the **Cross Spring** (*Křížový pramen*), is housed in an immense, domed granite building at the northern edge of the town. Adjacent to it is the attractive **Colonnade** (*Kolonáda*), a graceful cast-iron arcade that has a Neo-Baroque pavilion at either end, **53**

The graceful wrought-iron Colonnade overlooks Mariánské Lázně's Singing Fountain.

the Karolínin Spring. Uphill to the left is the unusual **Church of the Assumption**, octagonal in plan and Neo-Byzantine in style (built between 1844 and 1848), and above it is the heart of the original resort, **Goethe Square** (*Goethovo náměstí*), lined with elegant facades. At the right-hand end is the Hotel Kavkaz, originally the Weimar Hotel, which was the favoured haunt of King Edward VII. In the centre of the square is the **Spa Museum**, which occupies the house where Goethe stayed during his final visit in 1823.

The intellectual tone of the old days is maintained in the annual Chopin Summer Music Festival, while wooded hills around the town are criss-crossed with well-signposted walking trails. Nearby you will find the Czech Republic's finest **golf course**, founded by Edward VII in 1905.

built in 1889. It overlooks the modern **Singing Fountain**, whose water jets (illuminated with coloured lights after dark) dance in time to a recording of classical music (performances take place every two hours, on the hour, 7am to 9pm).

Beyond the fountain, there is a pretty garden walk that leads to another (non-singing) fountain, and a graceful Neo-**54** Classical colonnade sheltering

South Bohemia

The region to the south of Prague is a great basin drained by the River Vltava and its tributaries, the Otava to the west, and the Lužnice to the east. The wooded hills of the Šumava, where the Vltava and Otava rise, have for centuries marked the southern boundary of the Bohemian kingdom, and countless castles defend the natural north-south route into Austria. The eastern part of the region, called the Třeboňsko, presents a unique landscape of marshes and medieval fishponds, now protected within a national park.

Main attractions for visitors here are the castles of Český Krumlov, Hluboká, Jindřichův Hradec, and the forests and lakes of the Šumava.

ČESKÉ BUDĚJOVICE

The principal town of South Bohemia is České Budějovice (Budweis in German), which was founded by Přemysl Otakar II in 1265. It bears the distinction of having been one of the termini of the first ever horse-drawn railway in Europe (the other was Linz, Austria), which began operations in 1832, the horses giving way to steam locomotives in 1871. Today České Budějovice is an industrial city with a population of 97,000, famous as the home of *Koh-i-noor* pencils

The Two Buds

The famous American beer called Budweiser was first brewed in St Louis in 1876 by Adolphus Busch, an immigrant from Bohemia. Busch borrowed the name from the Budvar brewery in České Budějovice (known in German as Budweis), where he had once been an employee. The original Budvar beer is still made in České Budějovice, and is a far stronger and tastier brew than its American namesake.

55

This door handle at Hluboká depicts the gruesome emblem of the Schwarzenberg family.

Fountain of 1727. In the south-west corner stands the **Town Hall**, a 16th-century Renaissance structure that was given a Baroque facelift in 1730. Diagonally opposite is the 17th-century Cathedral of St Nicholas, and the rather grim-looking **Black Tower**, from the gallery of which you can enjoy a fine view of the town.

(since 1847), and Budvar beer (since 1894). (Budvar is better known by its German name, Budweiser – apart from the name, it bears no relation to the American 'Bud'.)

The focal point of the town is the immense **Ottokar II Přemyse Square**, one of the largest squares in Europe, each side measuring 133m (440ft). Around its edges are elegant arcaded buildings dating from the 18th and 19th centuries, and at its centre is the Samson

Hluboká nad Vltavou

About 10km (6 miles) to the north of České Budějovice lies the spectacularly sited castle of Hluboká, set on a hillside above the Vltava. A castle was first founded here in the 13th century, and changed hands several times before finally falling to the wealthy Bavarian Schwarzenberg family in 1661. In the 19th century the owners decided to convert this ancient fortress into their main residence, and had the entire building completely renovated in fashionable English Tudor Gothic style. The decorations are fantastically Disneyesque, resembling nothing so much as a child's crenellated toy castle.

As you pass through the main entrance, take a look at the huge bronze door handles fashioned in the shape of a Saracen's head with a crow pecking at his eyes. This is the Schwarzenberg family's grisly emblem, symbolizing their achievements in wars against the Turks, and it is a motif that you'll see repeated throughout the castle (look at the keyholes in the interior doors). The 60-minute guided tour leads you through a series of remarkable apartments, each with ornately carved wood-panelling on the walls and ceilings, impeccably polished parquet floors, family portraits and priceless 17th- to 18th-century tapestries.

Tábor

The town of Tábor, which lies about 60km (38 miles) north of České Budějovice on the road to Prague, played a key role in the Hussite Wars of the 15th century. It was here that Jan Žižka, the great Hussite military leader, established a stronghold in 1420, naming it after the biblical mountain in Galilee on which Christ was transfigured. Tábor served as a military base for the Hussites (religious and political reformers) until their defeat in 1434. A few militant radicals held on for another 20 years or so, but the town was finally taken by George of Poděbrady in 1452.

A statue of Jan Žižka stands beneath the church in the market square of Tábor.

The old town centre is fairly well preserved, and offers a pleasant hour's exploring. The town square, *Žižkovo náměstí*, hosts a lively market, watched over by a statue of Jan Žižka erected in 1884. Be sure not to miss the excellent **Hussite Museum** in the Town Hall (ask for an English text, as the explanations are all in Czech). Just inside the entrance you will see a reproduction of one of Jan Žižka's innovations – a peasant wagon fortified with wooden armour, mounted with a cannon – an ancient ancestor of the modern tank.

Třeboň

The attractive town of Třeboň stands at the centre of South Bohemia's Lake District. The region's picturesque ponds are not natural lakes, but a network of artificial fish-ponds, linked by a series of canals and sluices, that was created by the Rožmberk family in the 16th century for the breeding of carp (a staple of the Bohemian kitchen that traditionally forms the Christmas dish).

Třeboň lies on the north shore of the Svět fish-pond, one of the largest of the lakes. It has a tiny but beautiful old **town square**, *Masarykovo náměstí*, which is edged with arcaded houses in Baroque and Renaissance style, and a 16th-century Renaissance **château**, the home of bon viveur Petr Vok, last of the Rožmberks. He lived here from 1602 until his death, from the effects of excessive good living, in 1611. After Vok died the town came into the possession of the Schwarzenbergs, who erected a Neo-Gothic **mausoleum** in the park on the south shore of the lake. Both the Svět and the adjacent Opatovický ponds have beaches that are suitable for bathing.

Jindřichův Hradec

Like Třeboň, the town of Jindřichův Hradec sits on the shores of a large fish-pond. It was established in the early 13th century by Jindřich, the founder of the Jindřichův Hradec arm of the Rožmberk family. The Lords of Hradec,

as his descendants came to be known, were a powerful force in medieval Bohemia, holding positions of high office in the Royal Court. Their elevated standing was reflected in the opulent **castle** they created here, a Gothic structure that was considerably enlarged and rebuilt in Renaissance style in the 16th century. The castle has undergone more recent renovation, and is now one of the country's top attractions.

There are three separate guided tours on offer, each of which takes about 60 minutes. The first, Tour A, covers the **Adam Rooms**, a series of

The village of Rožmberk lies on the banks of the River Vltava, beneath the castle hill.

sumptuous Renaissance apartments with beautiful, painted wooden ceilings, built in the 16th century for Adam II of Hradec, the Lord Chancellor of Bohemia. Tour B takes in the old Romanesque-Gothic palace and the medieval castle kitchens, and Tour C explains the historical and architectural development of the castle, and includes a visit to the famous **59**

Rondel. You have to purchase a separate ticket to visit the castle's Black Tower.

The highlight of the old Gothic palace (Tour B) is a **Ceremonial Hall** whose walls are decorated with original 14th-century frescoes, which depict in gory detail the life of St George. The person who commissioned the paintings, Oldřich III of Hradec, appears to the left of one of the Romanesque portals, bearing the Hradec arms of a golden rose on an azure field. Also on this tour is the fascinating medieval **kitchen**, complete with original implements.

Tour C includes a visit to one of Europe's most unusual Renaissance buildings. Known as the **Rondel**, this garden pavilion was constructed in the 1590s. It was designed by the Italian architect Baldassare Maggi, with a circular ground plan and a steeply pitched conical roof. The interior is richly decorated with gilded stucco. In the 18th century musicians played in a cellar under the pavilion, and their music rose up to the concert hall above.

60

ČESKÝ KRUMLOV

Nestling in a broad loop of the Vltava River, and guarded over by a Renaissance castle, Český Krumlov well deserves its reputation as Bohemia's most beautiful town. The castle was founded by the Krumlov branch of the Vítkovec family in the 13th century, but when their line died out in 1302 the town was taken over by their relatives, the Rožmberks, who made Český Krumlov the administrative centre of their vast estates. They also enlarged and rebuilt their castle on a grand scale, making it the largest castle complex in the country outside Prague. When the Rožmberk line died out in the early 17th century, the castle passed into the possession of the Habsburgs and the Eggenbergs, and finally to the Schwarzenbergs in 1715.

Český Krumlov Castle is sited in a superb position along a rocky ridge overlooking the river and the Old Town. You enter via a bridge over a bear pit, and arrive in a courtyard which is dominated by the striking **round-tower**, with a colourful Renaissance gallery built in the 1580s. The view from the gallery is magnificent (separate admission fee). You continue through a second passage into a smaller courtyard, where tickets for the guided tour are available. The highlights of the tour include the attractive 16th- to 17th-century Rožmberk apartments, a beautiful rococo cabinet-room with a brightly coloured porcelain chandelier, a huge gilded carriage that was once used to carry gifts to the Vatican, and a superb 18th-century **ballroom**, whose walls are covered with amusing trompe-l'œil paintings of a masked ball (the artist has included a

The Land of the Rose

The Vítkovec family, which dominated South Bohemia in the 13th-17th centuries, was descended from Vítek of Prčice, an important Bohemian prince of the late 12th century. Legend has it that Vítek divided his estates among his four sons, and assigned to each a variation on his own heraldic emblem, a five-petalled rose. The three main branches were: the Lords of Hradec (gold rose on an azure field), Rožmberk (red rose on a silver field), and Třeboň (silver rose on a red field). The Krumlov branch died out in 1302, and their estate passed to the Rožmberks, who became so powerful that the entire family was often referred to as Rožmberk rather than Vítkovec.

Such was the extent of Rožmberk influence in the south that the region became known as The Land of the Rose, and their towns were called the Rose Towns. The heraldic rose can be seen in several of the region's churches, monasteries or castles. The last of the direct male line, Petr Vok Rožmberk, died in 1611, and the Rožmberk possessions passed into other hands.

61

*C*rowds gather in the Renaissance courtyard of Český Krumlov Castle.

spire that belongs to the 15th-century **Church of St Vitus** (*kostel sv. Víta*), which houses an ornate sepulchre dedicated to Vilém, one of the Rožmberk lords from the 16th century (see p.61). The Vltava, which almost encloses the Old Town in a sweeping bend, is very popular with canoeists, who entertain crowds of tourists with their attempts at shooting the weir below the castle.

portrait of himself, sipping coffee in one of the window niches). After the tour, you can cross over a lofty covered bridge between the castle rock and a neighbouring hill to visit the castle gardens, which contain an attractive 18th-century rococo **theatre**.

You must then retrace your steps and descend to the river to visit the superbly preserved **Old Town**, which in 1992 was given the status of a UNESCO World Heritage Site. Soaring over the huddle of medieval **62** buildings is the needle-like

ŠUMAVA

The forest-clad slopes of the Šumava hills, which form the natural border between the Czech Republic and Austria and Germany, stretch for about 125km (80 miles) along the southwestern fringes of Bohemia. The region was for many years a no-man's land – a closed border area in the shadow of the Iron Curtain.

Since the Velvet Revolution the region has been opened up, and the lakes and forests now provide good opportunities for outdoor sports enthusiasts.

Lake Lipno

A dam across the headwaters of the Vltava has created Lake Lipno, the Czech Republic's largest body of water. Its northern shore is fringed with campsites and beach resorts, while along its southern shore, which was a restricted military zone during Communist rule, there are trails for hiking. The lake offers bathing, boating and windsurfing.

Vyšší Brod

From Lipno dam the road follows the river along a winding valley to the village of Vyšší Brod (see p.4). This was the site of the founding of a Cistercian monastery in 1259 by Vok of Rožmberk, after he was miraculously rescued from the raging river by the intervention of the Virgin Mary. The monastery remained in service until 1950, when it was closed by the Communist regime, but it has recently been returned to the Cistercian order and is in the process of being restored.

The tour begins with the monastery **church**, which was built in the 14th century, but was greatly altered during the Baroque period and again in the 19th century. The high Gothic vault encloses a fine Baroque altar, adorned with a painting of the Assumption (as at all Cistercian monasteries), with statues of saints, and with the coat of arms of the Rožmberk family (a red rose on a silver field). The painting to the right depicts Vok's miraculous rescue from the Vltava, and that to the left shows Vok dedicating the monastery to the Virgin, while the first monks arrive behind him. In the south transept is the **Chapel of the Virgin Mary**, which contains a copy of the famous *Vyšší Brod Madonna* (the original is in the Convent of St George in Prague Castle); Vok is shown kneeling in the lower left-hand corner. The chapel in the north **63** transept contains the tomb of Petr Vok, a descendant of the monastery's founder, and the last of the Rožmberk line.

You then go into the cloister to visit the Gothic **chapter house** (13th century), which has four triple-rib vaults supported on a central pillar. The far wall has its original rose window tracery, with 19th-century stained glass. The final part of the tour takes you upstairs to the picture gallery, thence to the **library**, whose Philosophical and Theological Halls have beautiful rococo bookshelves made by one of the monks. The frescoes on the ceiling depict the Judgement of Solomon and the young Jesus preaching in the temple.

 Rožmberk nad Vltavou

Perched scenically on a rock above the Vltava, **Rožmberk Castle** is the ancestral seat of the Rožmberk family. Though the Rožmberks moved to Český Krumlov in 1302 they maintained an interest in their former home, and during the 16th century transformed it into an elegant Renaissance château. When the last of the Rožmberks died in 1611, the castle passed into the hands of the Schwarzenbergs, and later to the Boucquoy family.

The tour of the castle takes in several grandiose rooms. The **Rožmberk Hall** contains mementoes of the castle's founder. There's also a portrait of Perchta of Rožmberk, the so-called 'White Lady' who is said to haunt Český Krumlov Castle and other Rožmberk houses. Portraits and coats of arms of crusading leaders are contained in the **Crusaders' Gallery**, redecorated by the Boucquoy family in Neo-Gothic style with a wooden truss roof. The highlight is the early 17th-century **Knights' Hall**, which has a colourful wooden ceiling and paintings depicting the planets. Behind an iron grille is a fresco of Hephaistos and Hercules with a band of musicians, which is studded with real jewels. Just before you leave the hall, take a peek behind the stove, where the figure of Death secretly lurks behind a painted curtain.

A Selection of Hotels and Restaurants in the Czech Republic

Recommended Hotels

The hotel scene in the Czech Republic has improved greatly in the last five years. The shortage of rooms in Prague has been eased, but prices have soared, making it as expensive to stay in as any western European capital. In the rest of the country (except for Karlovy Vary and Mariánské Lázně), room rates are very reasonable. Old hotels have been renovated, and many new ones have been built, usually to a high standard.

It's advisable to book for hotels in Prague and Karlovy Vary, especially in summer and during festivals. Hotel prices usually include breakfast, and in the spa towns of Western Bohemia a spa tax of about 15 Kč is added on. As a basic guide we have used the symbols below to indicate prices for a double room with bath, including breakfast:

▍▍▍▍	over 3,500 Kč
▍▍▍	2,500-3,500 Kč
▍▍	1,500-2,500 Kč
▍	below 1,500 Kč

PRAGUE

Ametyst ▍▍▍
Jana Masaryka 11
Prague 2
Tel. (02) 691 17 58
Fax 691 17 90
86 rooms. Bright, modern hotel in attractively refurbished building situated just a short walk south of Wenceslas Square, and 5 minutes from Metro station I. P. Pavlova (Line C). All rooms have TV and private bathroom. Parking, sauna and fitness centre.

Atrium ▍▍▍▍
Pobřežní 1
Prague 8
Tel. (02) 24 84 11 11
Fax 24 81 18 96
788 rooms. Although this is the largest hotel in the country and looks like an office block, it still exudes a certain charm. The rooms are set around a huge marble-clad atrium, overhung with plants and echoing to the splash of fountains. Business and conference facilities, sauna, solarium, fitness centre, swimming pool and tennis courts.

Central

Rybná 8
Prague 1
Tel. (02) 24 81 20 41
Fax 232 84 04

90 rooms. Old-fashioned hotel in a quiet street a few minutes' walk from Old Town Square. Rooms are plain but clean with private bathrooms. Restaurant and bar.

Diplomat

Evropská 15
Prague 6
Tel. (02) 24 39 41 72
Fax 24 39 42 15

384 rooms and suites. Located about 3km (2 miles) from Prague city centre, though easily reached by Metro. The hotel is equipped to receive travellers with disabilities, with wheelchair access and five specially adapted rooms. Other hotel services include a gourmet restaurant, bar and nightclub.

Esplanade

Washingtonova 19
Prague 1
Tel. (02) 24 21 17 15
Fax 24 22 93 06

63 rooms. A small, elegant hotel, dating originally from the 1920s, which is set in a good central location near the National Museum just off Wenceslas Square. The restaurant is held in high esteem.

Grand Hotel Evropa

Václavské náměstí 25
Prague 1
Tel. (02) 24 22 81 87
Fax 236 52 74

89 rooms and suites. An extremely well-preserved architectural landmark, with splendid Art Nouveau decor that dates from 1889. The hotel overlooks Wenceslas Square, and has retained its original wood-panelling, light-fittings, stained glass and tilework. The somewhat genteel café is an excellent place to soak up local atmosphere.

Hotel Forum Praha

Kongresová 1
Prague 4
Tel. (02) 61 19 11 11
Fax 61 21 16 73

531 rooms. Modern tower block of gleaming glass and marble, next to Vyšehrad Metro station (Line C), a 5-minute ride from Old Town. Luxury rooms with private bathrooms, 24-hour room service.

Hotel Paříž

U Obecního domu 1
Prague 1
Tel. (02) 24 22 21 51
Fax 24 22 54 75

96 rooms and 2 suites. A gem of Neo-Gothic architecture and Art Nouveau decoration, built in 1907. Good location in the Old Town. **67**

Jalta Praha ▐▐▐▐

Václavské náměstí 45
Prague 1
Tel. (02) 24 22 91 33
Fax 24 21 38 66

89 rooms. A small, old-fashioned but luxurious hotel overlooking Wenceslas Square. The restaurant specializes in Czech cuisine and Moravian wines; terrace bar, and casino. Conference hall, meetings rooms, and business facilities.

Karl-Inn ▐▐

Šaldova 54
Prague 8
Tel. (02) 24 81 17 18
Fax 24 81 26 81

156 rooms and suites. A very comfortable hotel situated out in the suburb of Karlín, nor far from the Křižikova stop on Metro Line B. Facilities include car park, hotel bus, and wheelchair access.

Kavalír ▐▐

Plzeňská 177
Prague 5
Tel./fax (02) 52 44 23

49 rooms (five with wheelchair access). A comfortable and friendly hotel, 3km (2 miles) from the city centre on the main E50 highway towards Plzeň. Facilities include garage, private bathrooms and satellite TV. Tram runs from the hotel door to Wenceslas Square.

Palace ▐▐▐

Panská 12
Prague 1
Tel. (02) 24 09 31 11
Fax 235 93 73

125 rooms and suites. This is one of central Prague's most exclusive hotels, situated just off Wenceslas Square. Formerly patronized by European aristocracy, the building was refurbished in 1991 in a more or less happy mix of traditional, modern and Art Nouveau styles.

President ▐▐

Náměstí Curieových 100
Prague 1
Tel. (02) 231 48 12
Fax 231 82 47

90 rooms and suites. With its central riverside location, this hotel offers spectacular views of Prague Castle. Restaurants, bars, nightclub, terrace bar and casino.

Splendid ▐▐–▐▐▐

Ovenecká 33
Prague 7
Tel. (02) 37 33 51
Fax 38 23 12

35 rooms. A small, comfortable hotel situated in a delightful street not far from the Prague Exhibition Grounds. Nearby tram line (no. 26) takes you across the river into the Old Town. Rooms have TV and private bathroom.

Ungelt
Štupartská 1
Prague 1
Tel. (02) 24 81 13 30
Fax 231 95 05
In a secluded spot just behind Old Town Square, this is an exclusive hotel with 10 airy rooms, some of which have fine wooden ceilings.

U Raka
Černínská 10
Prague 1
Tel. (02) 35 14 53
Fax 35 30 74
5 rooms. An intimate hotel that has been charmingly renovated, conveniently located within easy walking distance of Prague Castle.

U Tří Pštrosů
Dražického náměstí 12
Prague 1
Tel. (02) 24 51 07 79
Fax 53 61 55
18 rooms. Just beside the Charles Bridge, this family-run hotel is one of the best in Prague.

U Zlaté Studně
Karlova 3
Prague 1
Tel. (02) 22 05 93
Along the former 'royal road', this Renaissance hotel has just two apartments, with parquet floors and period furniture throughout.

KARLOVY VARY

Bristol Lázeňské Sanatorium
Sadová 19
Tel. (017) 21 35 14
Fax 266 83
92 rooms. Comfortable retreat that offers spa treatment, medical and dental treatment, sauna, fitness centre, swimming pool, hair salon, and an excellent restaurant (which can cater for special diets).

Grand Hotel Pupp
Mírové náměstí 2
Tel. (017) 20 91 11
Fax 322 40 32
270 rooms. Large, luxurious hotel in a beautiful setting, offering very stylish accommodation and good facilities. A sprawling Baroque mansion, the hotel was established in 1701, and was a favourite haunt of European royalty. Gourmet restaurant, cocktail bar and casino.

Hotel Dvořák
Nová louka 11
Tel. (017) 241 45
Fax 228 14
87 rooms. Managed by Austrians, this hotel offers a high standard of accommodation within an historic building. The restaurant is highly rated. Facilities include sauna, spa centre and fitness room.

69

Motel Gejzír Park Pupp ‖

Slovenská 9
Tel. (017) 251 01
Fax 252 25
64 rooms. A drive-in motel and campsite which is situated just a few kilometres out of town. The old-fashioned rooms are pleasant enough, and have TV and private bathrooms. Restaurant, snack bar and swimming pool.

Puškin ‖–‖

Tržiště 37
Tel. (017) 322 26 46
Fax 322 41 34
40 rooms. This beautifully refurbished building right in the heart of the spa, overlooks the Sprudel geyser. Rooms have private bathrooms, and there is an attractive outdoor dining terrace.

MARIÁNSKÉ LÁZNĚ

Palace ‖‖‖

Hlavní třída 67
Tel. (0165) 2222
Fax 4262
48 rooms. An old-fashioned hotel with splendidly old-fashioned service to match. It has recently been refurbished in Italian style, with the best rooms overlooking the town's main square. Choice of two restaurants, one specializing in Czech cuisine, the other French.

PLZEŇ

Central ‖

Náměstí Republiky 33
Tel. (019) 22 67 57
Fax 22 60 64
69 rooms. From the outside this hotel appears to be a characterless concrete building, but the rooms inside are surprisingly comfortable, and each has its own private bathroom and TV. Good location right on the main square of Plzeň.

Panorama ‖

V lomech 11
Tel. (019) 53 43 23
Fax 53 43 28
25 rooms. A bright, modern hotel in an attractive location on the edge of town. Rooms have private bathroom, TV and video. There is ample parking space. The hotel also has a restaurant, sauna and a fitness centre.

ČESKÉ BUDĚJOVICE

Bakalár ‖

Masarykova 69
Hluboká nad Vltavou
Tel./fax (038) 96 55 16
11 rooms. A small, attractive hotel set in the little town below the imposing mass of Hluboká Castle. The hotel also has a restaurant that enjoys a good reputation.

Motel Dlouhá Louka

Stromovka 8
Tel. (038) 731 17 57
Fax 531 41
50 rooms. Motel and campsite on the southern edge of town, beside the road to Český Krumlov. Old-fashioned rooms with bathroom and black-and-white TV, but good value. Breakfast included.

Zvon

Náměstí Přemysla Otakara II
Tel. (038) 731 13 83
Fax 731 13 85
83 rooms, some with wheelchair access. Set in lovely historic building overlooking the main square. Comfortable rooms with private bathroom and TV. Cheaper rooms have shared bathroom facilities.

ČESKÝ KRUMLOV

Růže

Horní 153
Tel. (0337) 22 45
Fax 38 81
55 rooms. This hotel is housed in the former Jesuit College in the Old Town, next to the Church of St Vitus, and overlooking the river. Most rooms have their own private bathrooms and some have superb views over the surrounding area. Restaurant and bar. Horse-riding and fishing trips can be arranged.

TŘEBOŇ

Petra Voka

Holičky 40
Tel./fax (0333) 4000
30 rooms. A comparatively recent motel, located on the Vienna highway just south of town. The rooms are bright and modern rooms, and there's also a very lively bar and restaurant.

Regent

Lázeňská 1008
Tel. (0333) 42 51
Fax 42 53
42 rooms. Although it looks like an unappealing tower block from the outside, don't be put off. This is in fact a very comfortable hotel, in a good location next to a fine beach on the lakeside.

BRNO

Austerlitz

Táborského nábřeží 3
Tel. (05) 43 21 47 18
Fax 32 21 51
32 rooms. This hotel is managed by Best Western, and offers all the home comforts you would expect from this respected chain, including bar, restaurant and conference facilities. It benefits from a good central location next to the city's trade fair grounds.

71

Myslivna

Nad Pisarkami 1
Tel. (05) 38 32 47 56
Fax 43 22 00 12

If you have a car, you can escape to this rural retreat on a wooded hilltop to the west of the city. Cosy modern rooms all have private bathroom and TV. Restaurant and bar. For walking and fitness fans, there are also hiking and jogging trails nearby.

Slavia

Solniční 17/15
Tel. (05) 42 21 50 80
Fax 42 21 17 69

102 rooms. Central location, a few minutes' walk from Brno's main square at náměstí Svobody. All rooms with private bathroom and TV. Restaurant, café and bar with garden terrace.

BRATISLAVA

Danube

Rybné námestie 1
Tel. (07) 34 08 33
Fax 999

One of the city's newest and most luxurious hotels, located centrally on the river bank, next to the SNP Bridge. Rooms with private bathrooms and satellite TV. Esteemed restaurant and all the facilities you'd expect in a five-star hotel.

Turist

Ondavská 5
Tel. (07) 526 27 89
Fax 204 82 63

90 rooms. Comfortable modern hotel situated 2.5km (1.5 miles) northeast of the city centre. Tram no. 12 takes you to the centre in 10 minutes. Clean, bright rooms with private bathrooms and balcony. Restaurant and guarded car park.

HRADEC KRÁLOVÉ

Alessandria

Třída SNP 733
Tel. (049) 451 71
Fax 428 74

55 rooms. An old ČEDOK hotel located 2km (1 mile) northeast of the centre, easily accessible by tram. Old but comfortable rooms with private bathroom and TV. Friendly English-speaking staff; small parking area. Restaurant.

Černigov

Riegrovo náměstí 1494
Tel. (049) 69 01 11
Fax 329 98

150 rooms. Large, modern hotel block conveniently situated across the square from the railway station, and close to New Town shops and restaurants. Rooms with private bathroom and TV, restaurant, café, bar and disco.

MEZNÍ LOUKA

Mezní Louka

Mezní Louka
Tel. (0412) 981 89
35 rooms. An old-fashioned lodge set in the heart of the 'Bohemian Switzerland', one of the country's finest hiking areas. Good though basic accommodation only an hour's walk from the Pravčická brána rock formations.

ROŽNOV POD RADHOŠTĚM

Éroplán

Horní Paseky
Tel. (0651) 558 35
Fax 572 17
25 rooms, some of which have wheelchair access. Bright, modern motel on the eastern edge of town. More attractive than the Tesla, but more likely to be booked up. Rooms have private bathroom and TV. Parking and restaurant.

Tesla

Meziříčská 1653
Tel. (0651) 545 35
Fax 545 46
57 rooms. Rather sombre and gloomy, though rooms are clean and comfortable, with private bathroom and balcony. Facilities include restaurant, café and bar.

OLOMOUC

Gemo

Pavelčákova 22
Tel./fax (068) 286 25
28 rooms. A fairly new hotel set in a renovated historic building close to the main square. Rooms are comfortable and all have private bathroom, minibar and TV. Other facilities include car park, restaurant, café and bar.

Národní dům

ul. 8. Května 21
Tel. (068) 522 48 06
Fax 522 48 08
43 rooms. A 19th-century hotel in a central location not far from the town square. The hotel has been refurbished and the rooms are clean and comfortable, though a little old-fashioned, with private bathrooms. Good restaurant.

Prachárna

Kelovská 90
Tel. (068) 541 12 71
Fax 541 12 81
28 rooms. An attractive, modern three-star hotel which is located about 1.5km (1 mile) northwest of the city centre on the road towards Mohelnice. Rooms are built over the vaults of the old fortress; all have their own private bathroom and satellite TV. Good parking. **73**

Recommended Restaurants

Hundreds of new restaurants have opened up in the last few years. Prague especially sees new places opening every week, while others go out of business with similar regularity. Some are good, others are awful, and it is very difficult to keep up with the pace of change unless you actually live here. In Prague consult the *Prague Post* and *Velvet* (see Media, p.128), which carry regular reviews and listings.

Below is a list of restaurants recommended by Berlitz. We have concentrated on places that have been open for at least a few years, and can be relied upon to provide good service. It's advisable to make reservations for the upmarket restaurants.

As a basic guide we have used the following symbols to give an idea of the price of a three-course meal for two, excluding drinks:

▊▊▊▊	over 1,000 Kč
▊▊▊	700-1,000 Kč
▊▊	300-700 Kč
▊	below 300 Kč

PRAGUE

Cornucopia ▊
Jungmannova 10
Prague 1
Tel. (02) 24 22 09 50
Open 9.30am to 11pm weekdays, 10am to 10pm weekends. An American-style deli that serves an authentic selection of sandwiches, soups, salads and desserts. Good American breakfast served Monday to Friday, and brunch 10am to 4pm Saturday and Sunday.

Country Life ▊
Jungmannova 1
Prague 1
Tel. (02) 24 19 17 39
Open 8.30am to 6.30pm Monday to Thursday, 8.30am to 3pm Friday, closed weekends. Cafeteria-style self-service restaurant and wholefood shop that caters for vegetarians and vegans. Menu consists of simple sandwiches, salads, pizzas and tofu dishes. Also at Melantrichova 15 (just off Old Town Square).

The Globe

Janovského 14
Prague 7
Reservations not accepted
Open 10am to midnight. Lively and attractive though at times somewhat smoky American ex-pat café set in an English-language bookshop across the Vltava from the Old Town. Good coffee, and a delicious range of predominantly vegetarian sandwiches, quiches, salads, cakes and pastries.

Kavárna Meduza

Belgicka 17
Prague 2
Reservations not accepted
Open 11am to 2am. Delightful café a few minutes' walk from I. P. Pavlova Metro station. Furnished with antiques, it has a very relaxed atmosphere, and is frequented by a young and trendy crowd. Soups, sandwiches and pancakes.

Lisboa

Argentinská 1
Prague 7
Tel. (02) 684 51 97
Open daily 9am to 11pm. A lively and trendy eating place that has a Portuguese flavour, which means lots of seafood and chicken dishes, served with imaginative sauces and seasonings. Good selection of salads and desserts.

Molly Malone's

U obecního dvora 4
Prague 1
Tel. (02) 231 62 22
Open daily 11am to 12.30am. A welcoming Irish pub that serves Guinness on tap. The menu even includes Irish stew and colcannon, as well as a range of steaks. In Josefov, near St Agnes' Convent.

Monterey Mike's

Křížovnické náměstí 1
Prague 1
Tel. (02) 24 09 71 00
Open 11am to 11pm (bar till 2am). Lively and overcrowded Tex-Mex restaurant near the Old Town end of Charles Bridge, with a view of the Vltava. The menu of burritos, tacos, chimichangas and nachos complements the locally brewed Staropramen beer.

Na Rybárně

Gorazdova 17
Prague 2
Tel. (02) 29 97 95
Open noon to midnight Monday to Friday, noon to 4pm weekends. An attractive little fish restaurant, occasionally patronized by the President himself. Choose your own fish from the display, then have it weighed and cooked to order. The prices on the menu are per 100g (before cooking).

75

Nebozízek ▌▌▌–▌▌▌▌

Petřínské sady
Prague 1
Tel. (02) 53 79 05

Open 11am to 6pm and 7pm to 11pm. Closed Monday in winter. Take the funicular railway up to the top of Petřín Hill and enjoy the fine view from the garden terrace of this popular restaurant. The menu features a mix of Czech and international dishes. Reservations recommended.

Opera Grill ▌▌▌▌

Karolíny Světlé 35
Prague 1
Tel. (02) 26 55 08

Open 7pm to 2am. Small, intimate and luxurious restaurant, with a comprehensive menu including steaks, seafood and game, accompanied by fine wines and beers. Reservations essential.

Parnas ▌▌▌▌

Smetanovo nábřeží 2
Prague 1
Tel. (02) 24 22 76 14

Open daily noon to 3pm and 6pm to 11.45pm. Romantic, candlelit restaurant on the riverbank, with an attractive Art Nouveau interior. Great food, excellent service, and a good view of the castle. Popular Sunday brunch, with live jazz, served 11am to 2.30pm.

Pizzeria Kmotra ▌

V jirchářích 12
Prague 1
Tel. (02) 24 91 58 09

Open 11am to 1am. Lively café, with very popular pizzeria downstairs in the cellar. Long wooden tables and benches help create a friendly atmosphere. The huge pizzas, best eaten with a glass of the local beer, are excellent value. Close to the National Theatre.

Plzeňská Restaurace ▌

Na příkopě 17
Prague 1
Tel. (02) 22 08 06

Open daily 10am to 10pm. Good centrally located pub offering swift service and hearty helpings of goulash with dumplings. Rustic decor, reasonable prices and tasty Pilsner Urquell beer represent good value.

Principe ▌▌▌▌

Anglická 23
Prague 2
Tel. (02) 25 96 14

Open daily 8am to 3pm and 7pm to midnight. This exclusive Italian restaurant serves specialities such as veal scallopini, and uses only the freshest ingredients in all its dishes. Excellent atmosphere and attentive service. Reservations are advised for evening meals.

Red Hot and Blues   ▮▮–▮▮▮

Jakubská 12
Prague 1
Tel. (02) 231 46 39
Open 9am to 11pm. A bubbly and popular American-run restaurant offering a flavour of the Deep South, housed in the former king's stables. It draws Prague's sizeable expatriate community with dishes ranging from Louisiana Creole to Mexican and Texan specialities. There's live jazz most nights, and outdoor dining in summer.

Rhapsody   ▮▮▮▮

Dukelských hrdinů 46
Prague 7
Tel. (02) 80 67 68
Open 7pm to 2am, closed Sunday. A romantic restaurant and piano bar with mouth-watering French cuisine. Dishes include steak and salmon. This is a favourite haunt of high-powered business people and politicians, and reservations are highly recommended.

Rugantino   ▮–▮▮

Dušní 4
Prague 1
Tel. (02) 231 81 72
Open 11am to 11pm (from 6pm Sunday). Menu offers a range of 20 delicious pizzas baked in a wood-fired oven. There's also a small selection of pasta dishes.

Saté   ▮–▮▮

Pohořelec 152/3
Prague 1
Tel. (02) 53 21 13
Open 11am to 10pm. A pleasant Indonesian restaurant just down the hill from Strahov Monastery. The emphasis is on fairly spicy food, including pork and chicken satay (served with peanut sauce), *nasi goreng* (spicy noodles served with or without pork), special rice and prawn crackers. Fast service.

Shalom   ▮▮–▮▮▮

Maiselova 18
Prague 1
Tel. (02) 24 81 09 29
Open 12 noon to 10pm. A cosy and intimate restaurant in the heart of the Jewish Quarter, this is the only place in Prague that serves kosher food, located in the Jewish Town Hall community centre. Set menu lunch and dinner are good value. Reserve for dinner.

Taj Mahal   ▮▮▮▮

Škrétova 10
Prague 2
Tel. (02) 22 04 38
Open daily noon to 3pm and 6pm to 11pm. Located not far from the National Museum, on the opposite side from Wenceslas Square, this is one of the best of Prague's small selection of Indian restaurants. **77**

Thrakia

Rubešova 12/622
Prague 2
Tel. (02) 24 22 34 90
Open daily 11am to 11pm. This simple restaurant specializes in Bulgarian food, including pork goulash, chicken livers sautéed in wine, baked peppers, cucumber soup, and baklava.

U Malířů

Maltézské náměstí 11
Prague 1
Tel. (02) 24 51 02 69
Open 7pm to 10pm. An elegant French restaurant that is located in a 16th-century house with original painted ceilings. Menu of *haute cuisine* includes escargots, lobster, fish and game, accompanied by fine French wines. Very expensive. Reservations essential.

U mecenáše

Malostranské náměstí 10
Prague 1
Tel. (02) 53 38 81
Open daily 5pm to 11.30pm. A Gothic atmosphere, with period furniture, banners and pictures, and traditional Czech cuisine that includes stuffed duck and beef flambé, can be enjoyed in this Lesser Quarter restaurant noted for its excellent food and honest prices. Reservations essential.

U plebána

Betlémské náměstí 10
Prague 1
Tel. (02) 24 22 90 23
Open daily 11am to 11pm. In the old days of Communist rule, 'The Plebeian' was a favourite eating place of good party members. It now caters to upmarket business people who come to enjoy Czech specialities such as roast duck and mixed grill.

U zeleného čaje

Nerudova 19
Prague 1
Reservations not accepted
Open 10am to 7pm. An elegant tea-room and gift shop, used as a location during the shooting of the film *Amadeus*. The menu offers a tempting selection of teas, coffees and pastries. Get here early (there are only four tables).

U zelené žáby

U radnice 8
Prague 1
Tel. (02) 24 22 81 33
Open 6pm to midnight. The 'Green Frog' is just around the corner from the Old Town Hall, in a Gothic cellar. More of a wine bar than a restaurant, specializing in Bohemian and Moravian wines, with a selection of traditional Czech dishes to soak up the vino.

U zlaté studně 〓〓〓〓

Karlova 3
Prague 1
Tel. (02) 22 05 93
This intimate restaurant, whose name means 'At the Golden Well', is a Prague favourite. The historic setting in a Baroque town house is a perfect backdrop to traditional Czech cuisine, with mutton and *knedlíky* featuring strongly in the menu. The wines are particularly good. It is also possible to reserve a room here (see p.69).

U zlaté třináctky 〓

Nerudova 13
Prague 1
Tel. (02) 533 90 86
Open 9am to midnight. You'll find the 'Golden Thirteen' half-way up twisting Nerudova Street on the way to Prague Castle. It's a good place to take a lunch-break and to enjoy traditional Czech dishes such as goulash and dumplings.

Velkopřevorský mlýn 〓

Hroznová 3
Prague 1
Tel. (02) 53 03 00
Open 11am to 11pm. A secluded, romantic restaurant that enjoys a pretty situation just beside the mill stream on Kampa Island, off Charles Bridge. Very good value Czech cuisine.

Viola Trattoria 〓–〓〓〓

Národní 7
Prague 1
Tel. (02) 24 22 95 93
Open daily noon to midnight. An Italian restaurant in the heart of the Old Town, near the National Theatre. Nightly programme of jazz and poetry readings. Dinner reservations essential.

BRATISLAVA

Bystrica 〓

Most SNP (SNP Bridge).
Reservations not accepted
Open 10am to 8pm. This revolving restaurant at the top of the SNP Bridge's slanting tower has one of the city's best views. The menu is traditional Slovak, but if you don't want a full meal you can drop in for coffee and cakes.

Červený Rak 〓–〓〓〓

Michalská 26
Tel. (07) 33 13 75
Open 10am to midnight. 'The Red Crayfish' is located next to the old Pharmaceutical Museum. It is a bright restaurant in an Old Town basement, with a fresh approach to traditional Slovakian produce. Menu includes venison in red wine, wild boar, carp, and some vegetarian dishes. There is a patio in the adjacent Old Town moat. **79**

Pod Baštou ▮▮

Baštová 3 (off Michalská)
Tel. (07) 33 17 65
Open 11am to 11pm. In an out of
the way location down a narrow
alley near Michael's Gate, this
cellar restaurant has a real old-
fashioned feel, with vaulted brick
ceilings and wooden tables. It has
a wide range of local wines, some
drawn straight from the cask, and
a menu of classic Slovak dishes to
accompany them.

BRNO

Černý medvěd ▮▮

Jakubské náměstí 1
Tel. (05) 422 145 48
Closed Sundays. Set in the square
tucked beneath St James Church,
this is a small, intimate, and upmarket restaurant, serving a wide
range of international dishes as
well as classic Czech cuisine.

Oáza ▮

Veveří 10
Tel. (05) 73 45 42
Closed Saturday and Sunday. This
buffet-style restaurant, which is
situated just to the north of the Old
Town centre, offers a surprisingly
good selection of vegetarian food.
It's a good place simply for a
snack, but you can also have lunch
80 and dinner here.

KARLOVY VARY

La Belle Époque ▮▮▮▮

Grand Hotel Pupp
Tel. (017) 20 91 11
The superb Baroque dining room
in the Grand Hotel Pupp is one of
the republic's most impressive
restaurants. French menu, with
some Czech dishes. Reservations
and formal dress recommended.

Café Elefant ▮

Stará Louka 30
Tel. (017) 322 34 06
Elegant, old-fashioned café with
outside tables beside the river. A
perfect spot to enjoy coffee and
cream cakes.

Vinárna Karel IV ▮▮–▮▮▮

Zámecký vrch 2
Tel. (017) 322 72 55
Open 11am to midnight. Set atop a
tower built on the site of Charles
IV's original hunting lodge. The
terrace offers a good view over the
Market Colonnade below. Czech
and German/Austrian dishes.

Vegetarian ▮

I. P. Pavlova 25
Tel. (017) 290 21
Open 10am to 9pm. A welcome
retreat for non-meat eaters, on the
north side of the river upstream
from the huge Hotel Thermal.

North and East Bohemia

The northern part of Bohemia contains many of the mines, coal fields and heavy industries that brought prosperity to Czechoslovakia and made it one of the wealthiest nations in eastern Europe. Unfortunately, the legacy of this industrial wealth is the pollution that blights much of the region, in particular the Giant Mountains (Krkonoše) on the country's northeastern fringe, where acid rain has devastated large swathes of forest.

Despite this environmental damage, the north and east still contain some of the country's finest scenery, particularly in the spectacular rock towns of České Švýcarsko, Český Ráj and Adršpach-Teplice.

NORTH BOHEMIA

České Švýcarsko

Bohemia is ringed by hills, and the entire region drains ultimately into a single river.

The Labe (known as the Elbe once it crosses the border into Germany) has cut a narrow and steep-sided valley through a rocky massif on the Czech Republic's northern border, and all the waters of Bohemia eventually flow out through this gap. This massif is known as the Elbe Sandstone Hills (*Labské Pískovce*), and it provides fine hiking country and some impressive scenery.

The village of **Hřensko**, on the east bank of the Labe and only 1km (1,100yds) from the German border, is the lowest point in the Czech Republic (115m/380ft above sea level). The most scenic part of the Elbe Sandstone Hills lies to the east of Hřensko, centred on the village of **Mezní Louka**, which has a hotel, restaurant and campsite. Known as the Bohemian Switzerland (České Švýcarsko), this is a region of rocky escarpments and sandstone pinnacles, swathed in pine forests and criss-crossed by hiking trails. There are many possible walks that you can take, but the one described here takes in the highlights. **81**

Across the road from the Hotel Mezní Louka, follow the red-marked trail that leads off into the forest (it is signposted 'Pravčická brána 6km'). The path climbs through the trees, and then contours along the foot of a sandstone escarpment. Overhanging walls and bulging towers of fluted and honeycombed rock rise to your right, while through the trees to the left are views of forested hills. After an hour's walking you reach a junction, where a path winds up to the right to a restaurant tucked beneath the curve of the **Pravčická brána**, a natural sandstone arch on the edge of the escarpment. A metal staircase behind the restaurant leads up to other spectacular viewpoints.

Now go back down to the junction and continue on the red-marked path, which leads down to the road. Follow the road downhill for about 1.6km (1 mile) to a restaurant by a bridge, then continue along the green-marked nature trail that heads upstream along the riverbank and into the deep and narrow **Kamenice Gorge**.

There are two places where the gorge has been dammed, and boats ferry hikers up and down the river. Just wait at the landing stage for the next boat to come along (boats run daily from May to September, 9am to 6pm on the lower passage,

A boatman ferries walkers through the narrow, wooded defile of Kamenice Gorge.

till 5pm on the upper passage). The boatman punts you along with a long pole, and keeps up a constant and well-informed commentary on the surrounding rock features and wildlife. From the end of the upper passage, the path follows the river for 1km (1,100yds) then forks left up a small tributary stream to meet a blue-marked trail. Go left along this to return to Mezní Louka. (Total distance of the walk is 16km/10 miles; allow 5 hours including lunch break. Trainers are suitable footwear for the walk.)

Terezín (Theresienstadt)

The great fortress of Terezín was built in the 1780s in order to defend Habsburg Bohemia against the threat of Prussian invasion. The fortress, named after Empress Maria Theresa, never saw battle, but during the 19th century it became notorious as a political prison for the enemies of the Habsburg regime (one such was Gavrilo Princip, whose assassination of Archduke Franz Ferdinand at Sarajevo sparked off World War I). However, this notoriety pales into insignificance when compared with what happened here during World War II.

Following the occupation of the Czech Lands by the Nazis, a Gestapo prison was set up at Terezín in 1940. The next year a concentration camp was established, and Terezín began to play its awful part in Hitler's abominable 'Final Solution'. From 1941 until 1945, around 150,000 Jewish men, women and children passed through the gates of Terezín. The conditions were appalling, and many, especially the elderly, died here. Of the 87,000 who were transported from Terezín to the extermination camps of Auschwitz-Birkenau, Treblinka, and Majdanek, only 4,000 survived.

In the centre of the town, the **Ghetto Museum** (open daily 9am to 6pm) is a monument to the courage and spirit of the many thousands of Jews who suffered at the hands of the Nazis. The exhibits explain the history of the ghetto, which is powerfully represented in the drawings and paintings made **83** by the inmates, Nazi documents, displays of personal possessions, and transcripts of harrowing accounts of life and death in the camp.

The **Little Fortress** (*Malá pevnost*), on the edge of town, used to be the Gestapo prison. About 32,000 prisoners, most of them Czech resistance fighters, were incarcerated here, in crowded mass cells or in tiny solitary cubicles. The prison has been left as it was in 1945, and the self-guided tour leads you around the various cell-blocks and through an interminable underground passage to the place where some 250 inmates met their deaths at the hands of the firing squad.

A complete contrast to the horrific history of Terezín can be found just across the River Labe, in **Litoměřice**. Its town square is lined with attractive Baroque buildings, and the local art gallery contains one of the country's most important Renaissance masterpieces – the famous *Litoměřice Altarpiece*, painted in around 1500. It depicts scenes from Christ's Passion as well as the life of the Virgin Mary. A few miles northeast of the town is the stately home of **Ploskovice**, built in the 1720s, which has a splendid rococo interior with some magnificent painted ceilings, and a quaint grotto full of elaborate fountains.

EAST BOHEMIA

Hradec Králové

Hradec Králové, the capital of East Bohemia, is one of the country's oldest towns, lying at the junction of the ancient trade routes between Prague and Krakow in Poland, and from the Baltic to the Danube. In the 14th century it became the residence of the Bohemian queens (the town's name means Queen's Fortress), and it was later a stronghold in the battles between Prussia and the Habsburg Empire.

The **Old Town Square** sits above the confluence of the Orlice and Labe rivers. It is dominated by the 68m (223ft) **White Tower** (*Bílá věž*), built in 1574-80, and by the austere

Gothic **Cathedral of the Holy Spirit** (*chrám sv. Ducha*), founded in 1306. At the other end of the square is the superb **Gallery of Modern Art** (*Galérie moderního umění*), which houses a fine collection of late 19th- and 20th-century Czech art.

Across the river from the old town centre lies the **New Town** (*Nové Město*), which is something of a monument to modern Czech architecture. Built in 1900-30, its pleasing blend of decorative Art Nouveau and severe Functionalist design is best seen in pretty *Masarykovo náměstí*, a bright,

A massive Hussite chalice adorns a rooftop overlooking the town square of Litoměřice.

shop-lined plaza overlooked by pastel-shaded facades.

About 32km (20 miles) south of Hradec Králové lies East Bohemia's second city, **Pardubice**. It has a delightful Renaissance **town square**, *Pernštýnovo náměstí*, which is surrounded by fine 16th- and 18th-century buildings. One of these has a stucco facade that depicts Jonah and the Whale. **85**

Nearby is the 16th-century **castle**, whose ramparts have been converted into a pleasant public park. A museum and an art gallery are within the castle precinct. The town is known best for the **Great Pardubice Steeplechase**, Europe's most gruelling horse-race, which has been held annually since 1874 (2nd Sunday in October).

At the beginning of the 18th century, a Bohemian nobleman built a magnificent health resort on the banks of the Labe at **Kuks**, situated about 32km (20 miles) north of the town of

Hradec Králové. Count Franz Anton Sporck's intention was to create a Baroque spa that would rival Karlovy Vary in sophistication and splendour, and for a brief spell it did. Tragically, in 1740, the river burst its banks and destroyed many of the buildings as well as the mineral spring that was the spa's *raison d'être*. From that time, Kuks fell into decay, though it is now being restored as a tourist attraction.

The highlights of the guided tour include the 18th-century **pharmacy**, which has beautiful wooden shelves and tables painted to look like marble; the gorgeous Baroque chapel; and the old hospital, which houses 24 superb sculptures representing the **Vices and Virtues**, all by the prolific Baroque sculptor Matthias Braun. Copies of these statues adorn the terrace below the chapel, where the originals once stood.

About 5km (3miles) beyond Kuks is **Braun's Bethlehem** (*Braunův Betlém*), an open-air art gallery dedicated to the sculptor. Here, in a peaceful wood, Braun carved a number of large religious sculptures from natural sandstone boulders and outcrops, including depictions of the Nativity and the Journey of the Magi. (Braun's work can also be seen in Prague, notably four giant statues of Hercules on the Baroque front portals of the Clam-Gallas Palace.)

Český Ráj

The wooded hills and sandstone rocks of the Český Ráj, (Bohemian Paradise) which lie about 55km (35 miles) northwest of Hradec Králové, are a favourite weekend destination for work-weary Praguers. At the eastern end of the region lies the attractive town of **Jičín**, which has a beautiful, arcaded square overlooked by a Gothic gate-tower. It makes a good base for exploring the nearby **Prachov Rocks** (*Prachovské skály*), an area of sandstone pinnacles and escarpments similar to those in the České Švýcarsko (see p.81) and Adršpach-Teplice (see p.88). A 3km (1.8-mile) green-marked loop trail, which commences at the *Turistická chata* (Tourist Lodge), takes in all the scenic highlights.

Just a few miles northwest of Prachov lies the region's most prominent landmark. The ruined castle of **Trosky** teeters precariously on top of twin pinnacles of basalt, and its distinctive outline can be seen for several miles around. Visitors can climb to the castle walls for a stunning view over the surrounding countryside.

Giant Mountains (Krkonoše)

The Giant Mountains are so named not for their height – the Czech Republic's highest peak, Sněžka, is a modest 1,602m (5,260ft) – but for the mythical giant Krakonoš, who is said to inhabit the dense forests that cloak their lower **87** slopes. The mountains are not really spectacular, with broad, rounded summits, but they are nevertheless very popular with hikers, mountain bikers and skiers, and since 1963 the region's status as a national park has given it some protection. Unfortunately, this has not prevented the devastation of parts of the forest by acid rain.

The resort towns of Pec pod Sněžkou, Špindlerův Mlýn, and Harrachov are crowded with winter sports enthusiasts from January to early April, while in summer they are used as base camps by walkers and cyclists. The ski chairlifts continue to operate through the summer, carrying hikers and tourists to the mountain tops.

Adršpach-Teplice Rocks (Adršpašsko-Teplické skály)

The Adršpach-Teplice region, about 50km (30 miles) northeast of Hradec Králové and close to the Polish border, is the most spectacular of Bohemia's so-called rock towns, and its most attractive. A state

nature reserve encloses 25 sq km (6,180 acres) of thick pine forest and rugged hills, riven by deep valleys and soaring sandstone cliffs. It is perfect for rock-climbers, and is also popular with weekend hikers.

There are two main areas of rock towers, near the villages of Adršpach and Teplice nad Metují. The **Teplice Rocks** (*Teplické skalní město*) are reached from a car park beside the Orlík Hotel, from which a 7km (4.5-mile) blue-marked trail heads up a rocky valley. A 10-minute walk brings you to a flight of metal stairs and ladders that climbs to the **Střmen** pinnacles, the site of a 13th- to 14th-century wooden castle. You can see the sockets cut in the stone that once held the wooden beams.

The path continues up a valley lined with fluted sandstone crags to a climber's hut, beyond which you pass through an old stone gate. Here, just beneath the spectacular, sheer-sided, 100m (330ft) **Strážní věž** (Watch Tower), the path forks. Follow the left branch through even more dramatic rock towers, with names like *Chrámové náměstí* (Cathedral Square) and *Římské divadlo* (Roman Amphitheatre), before descending to a T-junction, where you turn right (still following the blue trail). The path leads into an immensely deep and narrow cleft in the rocks, called **Anenské údolí**. As the walls close in it becomes cooler and darker, with moss and ferns drooping from the walls. The final section of the chasm is so cool, even in summer, that it is known as **Sibiř** (Siberia). You finally emerge, blinking into the sunlight, back at the fork beneath the Watch Tower, from where you can retrace your steps to the car park.

At the **Adršpach Rocks** (*Adršpašské skalní město*) a few miles to the north, a green-marked trail loops among the pinnacles and canyons. It is shorter than the Teplice trail but far more strenuous as it involves a good deal of climbing and descending on wooden stairs and ladders. Another footpath links the two areas, and it is possible to combine the two in one long walk of about 16km (10 miles). An excellent hiking map is available from the ticket office at the entrance to the rocks. A pair of trainers is suitable walking gear for this trail, though you'll need to be fairly fit.

Sandstone pinnacles tower above the hiking trail at Toplice Rocks.

Moravia

The eastern third of the Czech Republic, which is separated from Bohemia by a range of low hills, is occupied by the ancient lands of Moravia, named after the Morava river, which rises near the Polish border and flows southward through the region to join the Danube at Bratislava. Moravia is renowned for the historic cities of Brno and Olomouc, the limestone scenery of the Moravian Karst, and for the museum of traditional wooden architecture at Rožnov pod Radhoštěm. It is also the area where most of the country's vineyards are to be found.

SOUTH MORAVIA

Brno

The Czech Republic's second city, and capital of Moravia, Brno is perhaps best known abroad as the host of the yearly Czech Motorcycle Grand Prix. But the city has also played an important part in Czech and European history. It withstood sieges by the Hussites in 1428 and by the Swedes in 1645, and in 1805 it was occupied by Napoleon's army before the French general's victory over the Austrians and Russians at Austerlitz (11km/7 miles east of Brno). Today it is a modern industrial city with a population of 400,000, although a few monuments to its former glory still survive.

The historic heart of Brno is the **Cabbage Market** (*Zelný trh*), a 13th-century square that continues to host a daily fruit and vegetable market. On the hill above the square rise the spires of the **Cathedral of St Peter and St Paul** (*katedrála sv. Petra a Pavla*), a Gothic building with a Baroque interior that houses a 14th-century sculpture of the *Madonna and Child*. Beneath the cathedral lies the **Moravian Museum** (*Moravské zemské muzeum*), whose exhibits cover the area's historical, archaeological and zoological points of interest. Off the east side of the square is one of the country's most gruesome attractions, the crypt of the **Capuchin Monastery** (*Kapucínský klášter*). On view to the public are the desiccated corpses and skeletons of erstwhile monks and aristocrats, which have been mummified by the dry air of the crypt, and which are now laid out on display in glass-topped coffins and communal vaults.

Brooding on a hilltop above the centre of the city is the grim fortress of **Špilberk**. The castle was founded in the 13th century, but most of the present structure dates from the 17th and 18th centuries, when it gained notoriety as a prison for the enemies of the Habsburg Empire. The casemates – long, vaulted chambers built within the ramparts – now contain a museum of prison life, while one of the castle buildings houses a museum devoted to the history of Brno.

The busy Cabbage Market lies at the historic centre of Brno, capital of Moravia.

To the north of Brno lies the **Moravian Karst** (*Moravský kras*), a region of wooded limestone hills famous for its caves and gorges. The main tourist centre is the village of Skalní Mlýn, near Blansko. From here you can join a tour of the fascinating **Punkva Caverns** (*Punkevní jeskyně*), part of which involves a boat trip along an underground river. The tour emerges at the bottom of a spectacular sink-hole, about 140m (460ft) deep, called the **Macocha Abyss** (*Propast Macocha*). You can reach the upper lip of the abyss by cable car, or by hiking up one of the many marked trails. The caves are very popular, especially in summer, when you may have to book a place on a tour several days ahead.

Another popular day-trip from Brno is to the mansion of **Lednice**, about 50 km (32 miles) to the south. The house was the country seat of the Liechtenstein family from the 14th century until 1945, and has been remodelled many times since, most recently in 1845-56, when it was given its present Neo-Gothic appearance. Highlights of the tour are the Library, with its elegant, wooden spiral staircase, and the Blue Ballroom, with its magnificent carved wooden doors and ceilings.

Telč

The little town of Telč lies on the far western border of Moravia, amid a landscape of low hills and lakes reminiscent of the Třeboňsko in adjoining South Bohemia. It sits on a finger of land surrounded by fish-ponds, clustered around one of central Europe's best-preserved and most beautiful town squares. The arcaded, cobbled precinct of **Zacharias Square** (*náměstí Zachariáše z Hradce*) contains not a single modern building to blight the brightly coloured parade of Renaissance facades.

At the west end of the square is the **castle** of Telč, owned by the Lords of Hradec from 1339 to 1712. It was Zacharias of Hradec, a 16th-century governor of Moravia, who erected the Renaissance palace you see today, using the Italian architect, Baldassare Maggi da Arogno, who was responsible for the reconstruction of the castle of Jindřichův Hradec (see p.58). The Renaissance apartments are probably some of the finest in the country: downstairs, you'll be shown the **Treasury**, with its trompe-l'œil *sgraffito* decoration, and **St George's Chapel**, which contains the tomb of Zacharias and his wife. Upstairs there is a fine **ballroom**, whose coffered wooden ceiling has 30 octagonal panels, each adorned with gilded reliefs of mythological figures.

The chapel of St George in Telč Castle contains the marble tomb of Zacharias of Hradec.

Vranov nad Dyjí

The castle of Vranov enjoys one of the country's most dramatic locations, poised high on a wooded crag overlooking the River Dyje. Originally it served as a military fortress guarding the southern borders of Moravia, but in 1680 it became the seat of the Althann family, who built the splendid Baroque mansion which now dominates the town. To reach the castle, cross the bridge over the river and leave your car in the car park halfway up the hill. From here it is a short walk uphill to the entrance.

The focal point of the castle is the **Hall of the Ancestors** (*Sál předků*), an immense oval chamber lit by large picture windows and oval skylights, and decorated with exuberant frescoes and statuary. Figures **93** around the sides represent the ancestors of Michal Jan II of Althann (who commissioned the hall in the 1690s), while the fresco on the huge, curved ceiling depicts the glorification of the Althann family (look for the family coat of arms, a red shield with a white horizontal band bearing a black Gothic 'A'). The guided tour carries on through a series of opulent late 18th-century apartments, including a beautiful marble bathroom with bronze taps in the shape of griffins' heads, and a room that was used as a Masonic Lodge – notice the Masonic motifs in the decoration: the pyramid, the compass and set square, the plumb line, and the Star of David.

In the neighbouring town of **Znojmo** is one of the Czech Republic's oldest architectural monuments, the 11th-century St Catherine's Rotunda, which contains a remarkable series of Romanesque frescoes. These were commissioned in 1134 and illustrate the genealogy of the Přemysl dynasty. You are not allowed inside the rotunda itself, but the adjoining castle

contains a museum that has a model of the church as well as photographs of the frescoes and details of the restoration and preservation work.

NORTH MORAVIA

Olomouc

Though long since surpassed in size by Brno and the coal-and-steel city of Ostrava, the city of Olomouc is historically the most important in Moravia. It was the capital of Moravia from 1187 to 1641, but it fell into decline after being sacked during the Thirty Years' War. Today it is a thriving industrial and university town, with an attractive city centre and many fine historical monuments.

The central square of *Horní náměstí* is dominated by the 70m (230ft) tower of the **Town Hall** (*radnice*). On one side is an **Astronomical Clock** that was restored after World War II by the Communist regime, which explains why the hours are marked by parading wooden workers rather than saints.

Next to the Town Hall is the tallest **Plague Column** in the Czech Republic, a tapering 35m (115ft) spire studded with elaborate Baroque statuary.

A short walk east along the city's main street brings you to the soaring Neo-Gothic spires of **St Wenceslas Cathedral** (*chrám sv. Václava*), on the site of the original castle of Olomouc. Beside the cathedral is the entrance to the **Přemysl Palace** (*Přemyslovský palác*), which contains some of the best-preserved Romanesque architecture in the country. After passing through a Gothic cloister decorated with 15th- to 16th-century murals you go upstairs to see a magnificent Romanesque arcade, all that remains of a bishop's palace built in the 1140s.

Olomouc was granted the status of bishopric in 1063, and the powerful Bishops of Olomouc acquired the nearby

town of **Kroměříž**, 35km (22 miles) to the south, as their country seat. They gave the town special privileges, and endowed it with some fine buildings and gardens. Most splendid of all is the huge Baroque heap of the **Bishops' Palace** (*Biskupský zámek*), built in 1690-1700. Its rather forbidding exterior conceals several remarkable rooms, in particular the immense rococo

*T*he Astronomical Clock in Olomouc town square is covered in motifs of the Communist era.

Concert Hall, with gilded stucco reliefs representing the arts, mathematics, architecture and hunting, and an enormous ceiling fresco depicting the apotheosis of the bishops.

In the hills to the northwest of Olomouc lies the decidedly sinister **Bouzov Castle**, which from 1799 to 1939 was the seat of the Grand Masters of the Teutonic Knights. Though founded in the 14th century, the castle was renovated in Neo-Gothic style in 1895-1910. A fascinating guided tour leads you through a series of restored apartments, the Grand Master's bedroom and office, the Hunters' Hall, and the basement kitchens, which are equipped with the latest culinary equipment from the turn of the century. Highlight of the tour is the **Knight's Hall**, which has an incredible wood-panelled, barrel-vaulted ceiling decorated with the sun and the stars, and elaborate wood-carvings on the walls and doors. To either side of the main door are carvings of St George and the Dragon, and a jousting knight, representing

respectively the spiritual and the worldly considerations of the Teutonic Knighthood.

Rožnov pod Radhoštěm

In the far east of Moravia is an attractive region of wooded hills. Wallachia (*Valašsko* in Czech) was settled in the 16th century by a tribe of semi-nomadic shepherds called the Vlachs who brought with them a distinctive folk culture and a tradition of wooden architecture which has been preserved in the famous **Wallachian Open-Air Museum** (*Valašské muzeum v přírodě*) at Rožnov pod Radhoštěm. The museum, which spreads over several acres of riverbank and hillside to the east of the town, contains many examples of wooden farmhouses, mills, churches and other buildings that have been transported from villages throughout Wallachia and reassembled here.

As you walk eastwards, away from the town centre, the first part of the museum that you come to is the **Wooden**

Town (*Dřevěné městečko*), with a church, a town hall, two taverns, several barns, and a collection of beehives carved out of tree trunks. You can wander around at your own pace, and enjoy a meal or a drink in one of the inns. The second part, **Mill Valley** (*Mlýnská dolina*), is a working museum of timber technology (accessible by guided tour only; 45 minutes). Here you can see a fulling mill (where felt is made), a flour mill, a saw mill, and a blacksmith's forge, all in full working order and all put through their paces as you look on.

The third part is called the **Wallachian Village** (*Valašská dědina*), and stretches uphill above the valley (guided tour only; 1 hour 45 minutes). The guide takes you on a stroll among barns and farmhouses, pausing at the vet's house, the windmill, and the schoolroom.

Traditional architecture and a working forge in Rožnov pod Radhoštěm's open-air museum.

97

Slovakia: Bratislava

Bratislava (Pressburg in German), the capital of Slovakia, sits astride the Danube only 56km (35 miles) downstream from Vienna, and 120km (75 miles) south of Brno. Bratislava and Brno are linked by a motorway, making the Slovakian capital a feasible day-trip from the Czech Republic (avoid weekends, as there may be long queues at the border).

Unlike the Czech Lands, Slovakia was for most of its history part of the Hungarian Empire, and from 1526 until 1784 Bratislava was actually the capital of Hungary. During the 18th century it was one of central Europe's most important cities and a leading cultural centre, home to the court of Empress Maria Theresa and the scene of performances by composers Mozart, Haydn and Beethoven. The city became industrialized in the 19th century, and is still a major river port and rail junction. It still has an important cultural role – it is home to the Slovakian National Theatre, the National Gallery, and Comenius University – and it is well known for its wine – it has over 1,000ha (2,500 acres) of vineyards within the city limits.

Modern Bratislava is a city of 450,000 people, but its historic centre is concentrated in a relatively small area on the north bank of the Danube, and the principal sights can easily be covered on foot in one day. Begin at the wide square of *Hurbanovo námestie* on the northern edge of the old town. From here you cross a bridge over the old moat and pass beneath the first of two towers that guard **St Michael's Gate** (*Michalská brána*). On the left look out for an old house called *U červeného raka* (At the red crayfish), which once served as a Baroque pharmacy and which is now home to a fascinating **Pharmaceutical Museum**. Beyond this is the second gate-tower, containing a museum of weaponry. From the battlements there is a fine view over the town.

Michalská Street stretches ahead, lined on either side with grand Baroque buildings and trendy modern cafés. Off to the left is the leafy **Main Square** (*Hlavné námestie*), once the main market-place. The beautiful **Old Town Hall** houses a museum illustrating Bratislava's history, and a smaller exhibition devoted to the city's wine industry. At the south end of Michalská (which changes its name at this point to Ventúrska), turn right along Panská Street to find the grim, Gothic hulk of **St Martin's**

The charming streets of Bratislava's old town; the city's pharmaceutical museum (below).

Cathedral (*Dóm sv. Martina*). Built from the 14th to 16th centuries, this modest church was the place where the royal heads of Hungary held their coronations; look at the tip of the spire, which bears a replica of the Hungarian crown.

Squatting on the hilltop just across from St Martin's is Bratislava's castle, which is reached by climbing a steep, cobbled street on the far side of the freeway. A distinctive **99**

*B*ratislava's castle offers a fine view of the Danube and the futuristic SNP Bridge.

wedge-shaped house at the foot of the hill contains an interesting **clock museum**, with examples of the horologist's art dating from the 15th to the 19th century. The **castle** itself is plain and forbidding, built on a square plan with a squat tower at each corner. Its grimly austere walls enclose a dour courtyard. Inside there is a museum of Slovakian history and archaeology. The main attraction, however, is the sunny park that spreads around the castle. It affords a breathtaking panorama of the River Danube and the striking SNP Bridge, a daringly modern structure that has a revolving restaurant at the top of its single tower. There's a splendid view from up here over three countries: immediately across the river and to your left lies Slovakia; directly to the south Hungary shimmers in the haze; finally, Austria is just a few kilometres away to your right.

What to Do

Shopping

Although not yet in the same commercial league as London, Paris and Rome, Prague can now claim to be a shopper's city. The range and quality of goods on sale has improved enormously in the years since the Velvet Revolution, and a number of small shops selling gifts, souvenirs, art, antiques and other speciality items have opened up. As well as the shops, there are street markets – there is a fruit and vegetable market in Havelská Street, just south of Old Town Square, and a huge one in Holešovice, on Bubenské Embankment, north of Štvanice island (Monday-Saturday). Most shops open from 8am to 6pm weekdays, with an hour-long lunch-break

The most famous manufacturer of Bohemian crystal is Moser of Karlovy Vary.

around 1pm, and from 8am to 1pm Saturdays. Shops catering to tourists open around 10am, and stay open on Sundays and in the evenings until 8 or 9pm.

Glass (*sklo*) and **porcelain** (*porcelán*). Bohemian crystal is found almost everywhere in the Czech Republic and is of extremely high quality. You can choose from a variety of articles, from tiny glass figures and engraved goblets, to large, decorated vases and elaborate chandeliers. All the principal

Locally produced pottery and porcelain are available in many Czech towns.

tourist towns are packed with glass shops. Besides the well-known Moser shop, the other outlets to look for are Crystal and Bohemia. Bohemian china and porcelain also make a very good buy, at prices far lower **102** than those found in the West.

Antiques (*antika*). Prague has always been a happy hunting ground for collectors of antiques. The streets of the Old Town and the Lesser Quarter contain many Aladdin's Caves packed with fascinating and desirable objects. Little shops are also beginning to appear in many of the more frequented tourist towns throughout the country. But beware, there are many fakes around. Even if you do stumble across some treasure, you may need to have an export licence to get it out of the country. You can obtain details from the shop, or from the Arts and Crafts Museum, 17 Listopadu 2, Prague 1 (opposite the Rudolfinum).

Handicrafts (*řemeslo*). Some traditional Czech crafts include wood-carving, basket-making, weaving, embroidery, jewellery and ceramics. There are shops and market stalls in most towns selling hand-made marionettes, dolls in regional costumes, wooden toys, baskets, painted wooden Easter eggs, and gold- and silverware studded with Czech garnets (a semi-precious stone which has a red-brown colour). Some shops also sell polished agates, fossils, and mineral crystals from the ore-bearing mountains that surround Bohemia.

Music (*hudba*). Cassette tapes and classical CDs, especially music by national composers such as Dvořák, Smetana, Janáček and Martinů, are a real bargain. Music shops can be found in every Czech town of any size.

Entertainment

Prague

Prague has a noble musical tradition, having nurtured the talents of Dvořák, Smetana and Janáček, and hosted performances and premieres by Mozart, Liszt, Tchaikovsky, Beethoven and Wagner. That tradition is celebrated in May in an annual feast of classical music in the Prague Spring Festival, with anything up to half-a-dozen concerts a day in summer. A monthly *Guide to Cultural Events* tells you what's on, and there are also entertainment listings in the *Prague Post* and *Velvet*, sold at newspaper kiosks in central Prague. Weekly listings are also displayed on posters at tram stops or metro stations.

Classical music, opera and ballet. Classical concerts are performed all year round, but especially during the Prague Spring Festival (see p.106) and the Mozart Festival (late June). There are brass band concerts on Saturdays at 10.10am, May to September, in the Na Valech Gardens; concerts at 12 noon on Tuesdays, Thursdays, Fridays and Sundays at 1pm, and Saturdays at 5pm (May until October) in the Lobkowicz Palace. Concerts may also be held on the staircase outside the National Museum. Other concert venues to look for include the Rudolfinum (Alšovo nábřeží 12, in the Old Town, tel. 24 89 31 11); the Spanish Hall (*Španělský sál*) in Prague Castle (tel. 24 53 34 74); and the State Opera (Legerova 73, tel. 24 22 98 98).

103

*P*rague's music and theatre can be enjoyed in many settings, both formal and informal.

Other music. Prague is also a major centre for jazz and rock, and the city has many smoky jazz basements as well as a thriving club scene. The city's Strahov Stadium is a regular venue for huge rock concerts staged by the likes of Pink Floyd and the Rolling Stones. **104** The Prague International Jazz

Festival is an annual event that takes place in October.

Theatre. Prague's best known and most accessible theatre group is the *Laterna Magika* (Magic Lantern), whose pioneering blend of music, mime, dance, film, and humour has been thrilling audiences since the 1950s. Prague also has an extensive programme of both traditional and experimental theatre, although most productions are in Czech.

Buying tickets. For the more popular events, you should book your tickets in advance (book in March for the Prague Spring Festival). You can buy tickets from the box office (stand-by tickets available the hour before the performance begins), from PIS (see Tourist Information Offices, p.135), through your hotel, or (more expensively) through one of the city's ticket agencies. Bohemian Ticket International (BTI) is a computerized network that offers tickets not just for music and theatre, but for sports events and rock concerts too. For telephone bookings tel. 24 81 40 20; for fax bookings contact 24 81 40 21; for postal bookings write to BTI, Salvátorská 10, Prague 1.

Outside Prague

Brno and Bratislava both have annual classical music festivals, and Bratislava also has an international jazz festival in September. Outside the major cities, cultural events are concentrated in the spa towns of West Bohemia, which have busy summer programmes of concerts and theatre. Karlovy Vary hosts an important International Film Festival in July, a Dvořák Music Festival in September, and a jazz festival in May.

One of the best known and most colourful events is the annual Folklore Festival held in July in Strážnice (60km/38 miles southeast of Brno), when groups from all over the Czech and Slovak Republics gather to celebrate traditional music and dance.

Calendar of Events

May	Jazz festival, Karlovy Vary.
12 May-2 June	Prague Spring Festival, various city venues. Major international classical music festival.
early June	International Folklore Festival in Hradec Králové and Pardubice.
June-July	South Bohemia Music Festival. Concerts in Třeboň, České Budějovice and Jindřichův Hradec.
July	Strážnice Folklore Festival.
	Mariánské Lázně Cultural Festival.
	International Film Festival, Karlovy Vary.
early August	Škoda Czech Open, international tennis tournament at Prague-Stvanice.
August	Český Krumlov International Festival. Music, theatre, dance, folklore.
late August	International Motorcycle Grand Prix, Brno.
	Chopin Festival, Mariánské Lázně.
early September	International Folklore Festival, Brno.
September	Prague Autumn Festival, Municipal House. International music festival marks beginning of concert and theatre season.
	Dvořák Music Festival, Karlovy Vary.
early October	Beer Festival, Plzeň.
October	Prague International Jazz Festival.

Sports

Hiking and climbing. The Czech Republic is criss-crossed by thousands of kilo-metres of marked hiking trails, all signposted and colour-coded, and shown on a series of excellent hiking maps (see p.128). The best walking areas are the Krkonoše, the Šumava, the Česкé Ráj and the Český Švýcarsko, and there is excel-lent rock-climbing to be had in Adršpach-Teplice and the Český Ráj. If you plan to tramp the high tops of the Krkonoše, be sure to take full hill-walking equipment – the weather can change suddenly, and snow-storms can occur, even in summer.

Cycling. A bicycle is an excel-lent way of exploring off the beaten track. Special bicycle routes are marked on the 1:50,000 hiking maps (see p.128), and with a mountain bike you can follow many of the low-lying footpaths too. Bikes can be hired in Prague and Karlovy Vary (see p.118).

C rowds often gather to watch canoeists shooting the weir at Český Krumlov.

Water sports. Canoeing is a favourite Czech pastime, espe-cially on the upper Vltava and Otava rivers in the region of South Bohemia. Canoe touring in two-seater kayaks or Cana-dian canoes is undoubtedly the most popular form of the sport – there is little white-water ac-tion to be had. Convenient riverbank campsites are found along the banks of the Vltava and Otava rivers. Canoes and inflatable boats are available for hire in Český Krumlov.

107

Still-water canoeing, wind-surfing, dinghy sailing and yachting can all be enjoyed on Lake Lipno, in the Šumava hills. Equipment can be hired at some of the tourist towns on the northern shore. There are bathing beaches all around the lake, as well as on many of the artificial ponds in the Třeboňsko region. Swimming and boating can also be enjoyed at Slapy Lake, 32km (20 miles) south of Prague.

Skiing. The mountains of the Czech Republic are not that high, but they enjoy a good covering of snow in winter, and skiing is very popular with the Czechs. Facilities and hire equipment are of a lower standard than in the Alps. The best downhill skiing is in the Krkonoše and the Šumava, and there are good cross-country trails in all the main mountain areas. The season lasts from December to April.

Golf. The Czech Republic's first golf course, at Mariánské Lázně, was founded in 1905 by Britain's King Edward VII,

and regularly hosts international tournaments. There are other courses at Karlovy Vary (founded 1934) and Karlštejn, the latter enjoying fine views of the nearby castle. All are open April-October.

Tennis. You can play tennis in Prague at the prestigious Štvanice Stadium, located on an island in the Vltava, downstream from the city centre, but you will have to book a court before you play (tel. 231 63 23). There are other courts in Prague, at Strahov and in the Letná Park.

Spectator sports. The most popular spectator sports in the country are football (September-December, March-June), ice hockey (September-April), basketball and volleyball. The principal sporting venue is Strahov Stadium in Prague, situated just west of the city centre. Horse-racing takes place on Sunday afternoons from May to October at the Velká Chuchle racecourse, about 5km (3 miles) south of Prague city centre.

Eating Out

Czech cuisine is based on hearty peasant fare, similar to that of neighbouring Austria and southern Germany, with the occasional spicy dish betraying a Hungarian influence. The best-known Czech dish is *knedlíky* (dumplings), served traditionally as an accompaniment to main courses in place of potatoes, rice or pasta. Most Czech main courses are based on meat – either slices of roast pork or beef with a cream sauce, or a rich, chunky stew; venison, wild boar, hare and duck are also popular.

Where to Eat

There is a wide variety of eating places, ranging from very expensive restaurants to cheap and cheerful snack bars. A *restaurace* is a conventional full-service restaurant, which may be exclusive or geared to a regional or foreign cuisine. You can also get full meals in a *vinárna* (wine bar), where the ambience is often intimate and possibly historic and folkloric as well; or a *pivnice* (beer hall), where the mood is likely to be jolly and the service informal. For simple coffee and cake, head for a *cukrárna* (the equivalent of a pâtisserie), and take your pick of the sticky, high-cholesterol cream cakes,

Hearty Czech meals are served in beer halls as well as in traditional restaurants.

pastries or gateaux; or go to a *kavárna*, an old-fashioned café that serves coffees, soft drinks, pastries and snacks.

For a simple snack, try a *bufet*, a stand-up, fast-food outlet that offers a selection of greasy delights, from hot dogs and hamburgers to humble potato cakes and deep-fried cheese. If you see a sign that says '*samoobsluha*', it means 'self-service'. (For a selection of recommended restaurants and cafés, see pp.74-80.)

Breakfast

In a typical hotel, breakfast (*snídaně*) is served between 7.30 and 9.30am and consists of cold ham and cheese, with rye bread or long, white rolls called *rohlíky*, usually washed down with coffee. In the more expensive hotels there will be a choice from an extensive buffet of cereal, fruit, sausage, ham, eggs, cheese, rolls and pastries. Since the working day begins early in the Czech Republic, you have the option of taking breakfast in a snack bar from around 5.30am.

110

Lunch and Dinner

For Czechs, lunch (*oběd*) is the main meal of the day, and is eaten between noon and 2pm; dinner (*večeře*) is usually little more than a light snack. In tourist hotels and restaurants, you can enjoy a full, three-course dinner from around 6.30 to 10 or 11pm. The menu (*jídelní lístek*) in tourist areas is normally in Czech, German and English; the farther afield you go, the more likely the menu will be in Czech only.

The traditional **appetizer** is Prague ham (*pražská šunka*), thinly sliced and served with cucumber and horseradish or gherkins. *Chlebíčky* are small open sandwiches of French bread, topped with cheese, gherkins, smoked fish or ham.

Soup (*polévka*) is the usual start to a Czech meal. Among the favourites are *cibulačka*, or onion soup, served with cheese and croutons, and *bramborová* (potato soup). Others include *boršč* (Russian beetroot soup), *hovězí* (beef broth), *hrachová* (thick pea soup), and *čočková* (lentil soup).

At Christmas, pride of place goes to carp (*kapr*). These **fish** have been bred in the fishponds of South Bohemia since the Middle Ages, and are eaten all year round, either fried (*smažený*) or oven-baked with caraway seeds (*pečený na kmíně*). Trout (*pstruh*), zander (*candát*), pike (*štika*) and eel (*úhoř*) are also popular.

When it comes to the **main course**, the local favourite is roast pork, dumplings and sauerkraut (*vepřové, knedlíky a zelí*). Another regular is roast beef with a sour cream sauce (*svíčková pečeně na smetaně*), served with dumplings and cranberries. Goulash (*guláš*) is a rich stew of pork, beef or venison with a paprika sauce. Wiener schnitzel (*vídeňský řízek*) is a thin cutlet of veal, fried in breadcrumbs. Side dishes are vegetables (*zelenina*), potatoes (*brambory*), or French fries (*hranolky*).

Tourists enjoy a coffee in the Art Nouveau atmosphere of Prague's Hotel Europa.

Czech **desserts** (*moučník*) are every bit as heavy as the main course. Plum dumplings (*švestkové knedlíky*) are served with icing sugar and melted butter, while *jablkový závin*, are whole apples stuffed with cinnamon and raisins, and baked in flaky pastry. If you fancy something less weighty, ask for *palačinky* (crêpes), which may be accompanied by ice cream (*zmrzlina*), stewed fruit (*kompot*), or a sticky chocolate sauce (*čokoládová*).

Vegetarians

The heavy emphasis on meat in Czech cuisine means that vegetarians will have to forego most traditional dishes; even the vegetable soups commonly use meat stock, and salads are often uninspiring. In Prague, some restaurants catering for vegetarians are in business, while more open every year. Non-vegetarian restaurants are increasingly offering dishes without meat. Outside Prague and other tourist towns, the Czech Republic is a nation of unreconstructed carnivores.

Snacks

The most popular of Czech snacks, available from street stalls in Prague and other large towns, is *klobása* (a thick pork sausage), served with mustard and a piece of rye bread. Other high-calorie delicacies include *smažený sýr*, cheese coated in breadcrumbs and deep-fried; *bramborák*, fried potato cakes with garlic and salami; and *párky* (frankfurters).

Drinks

The Czech national drink is **beer** (*pivo*) – the republic boasts the world's highest per capita beer consumption, at over 150 litres a year. Czech beer is widely recognized as the world's best, a reputation it has held for many centuries. In Plzeň local brewers used their soft water, hops from neighbouring Žatec, and a bottom-fermenting yeast to develop a pale, dry, highly hopped beer that became the standard for Pilsner beers throughout the world. The original and best, which has been brewed in Plzeň since 1842, is *Plzeňský* *prazdroj* (better known abroad as Pilsner Urquell). You can buy your beer bottled, but the best stuff comes from the tap – order a *malé pivo* (300ml) or a *velké pivo* (500ml).

The Czechs produce, and consume, far less **wine** than their neighbours in Slovakia. Vineyards are concentrated in South Moravia, with 14,000ha (35,000 acres) under the vine; Bohemia has a mere 500ha (1,200 acres), around the town of Mělník, north of Prague. Bohemian wines are similar to German ones, and the local preference is for a slightly sweet white (*bílé*). The reds (*červené*) are slightly better – look for Vavřinec, Frankovka and Rulandské.

The most renowned Czech **spirit** is *Becherovka*, served chilled as an aperitif, or mixed with tonic as a long drink. Others are *griotka* (cherry-flavoured), and *meruňkovice* (apricot brandy). *Slivovice* is a very pungent plum brandy.

For **non-alcoholic drinks** (*nealkoholické nápoje*), all the main western brands of soft drink can be found. The local

The Czech Republic is famous for its beer – this local brewery is in Znojmo.

mineral water is *Dobrá voda* – red top is fizzy, blue top is still.

Coffee (*káva*) is usually served black, with the grounds in a sludge at the bottom of the cup. A passable *cappuccino* is still hard to find. **Tea** (*čaj*) is simply a tea-bag covered with luke-warm water and served with a twist of lemon. **113**

To Help You Order...

Could we have a table?		**Máte prosím volný stůl?**	
The bill, please.		**Zaplatím.**	
I'd like…		**Prosím…**	
beer	**pivo**	meat	**maso**
bread	**chleba**	the menu	**jídelní lístek**
butter	**máslo**	milk	**mléko**
cheese	**sýr**	mineral water	**minerálku**
coffee	**kávu**	salad	**salát**
dessert	**moučník**	sugar	**cukr**
egg	**vejce**	tea	**čaj**
ice cream	**zmrzlinu**	wine	**víno**

...and Read the Menu

bažant	pheasant	**knedlíky**	dumplings
brambory	potatoes	**králík**	rabbit
drůbež	poultry	**kuře**	chicken
fazole	beans	**květák**	cauliflower
hotová jídla	main courses	**kyselé zelí**	sauerkraut
houby	mushrooms	**nápoje**	drinks
hovězí	beef	**polévka**	soup
hrášek	peas	**rajská jablka**	tomatoes
hrušky	pears	**ryby**	fish
husa	goose	**rýže**	rice
jablka	apples	**špenát**	spinach
játra	liver	**srnčí**	venison
jazyk	tongue	**studená jídla**	cold dishes
jehněčí	lamb	**šunka**	ham
kachna	duck	**telecí**	veal
kapr	carp	**vepřové**	pork
114 klobása	sausage	**zelenina**	vegetables

BLUEPRINT
for a
Perfect Trip

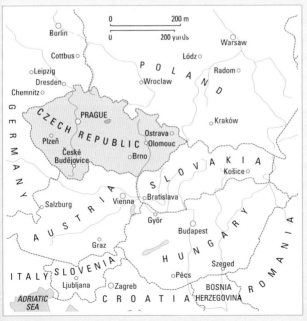

An A–Z Summary of Practical Information

Listed after many entries is an appropriate Czech translation, usually in the singular. You may find this vocabulary useful when asking for information or assistance.

A

ACCOMMODATION (*ubytování*)
(See also CAMPING on p.118, YOUTH HOSTELS on p.139 and the selection of RECOMMENDED HOTELS starting on p.65)

In the last five years there has been a considerable improvement both in the range and the standard of accommodation available in the Czech Republic. There has also been an explosion in the numbers of rooms for rent in private houses, as residents attempt to cash in on the tourist boom. In general, the standard of accommodation is good, and (outside Prague) inexpensive compared to western Europe. If you plan to stay in Prague, Karlovy Vary, Český Krumlov or other popular tourist towns in July and August especially, you are strongly advised to book your accommodation in advance. (Prague can be busy any time from April to November, particularly during festivals and conferences, and over the Christmas and New Year season.)

Hotels. These are graded in categories ranging from five stars down to one star. Most tourist hotel prices include private bathrooms and breakfast. In older hotels there may be two or three rooms sharing a single bathroom. Most hotels have a restaurant that serves dinner until about 10pm. A *Hotel Garni* has limited restaurant facilities and offers breakfast only.

Motels. Motorists can take advantage of the many new motels that have sprung up along the country's highways. These are usually bright, modern and reasonably priced.

Pensions and private rooms. One of the least expensive options for the visitor is to rent a room in a private Czech home. This is a little like a British bed-and-breakfast, where you may have to share the living room, bathroom and kitchen with the family. Accommodation agencies in Prague can book a private room for you. Elsewhere look for signs saying *Privat* (private) or *Zimmer frei* (vacancies).

In Prague, there are **accommodation agencies** at the airport, in the main railway station, and in the city centre. Try AVE (open daily 6am-11pm), at the airport and in the main railway station (*Hlavní nádraží*), tel. 24 22 32 36; ČEDOK, Na příkopě 18, tel. 24 19 76 15; or Pragotur/PIS, Staroměstské náměstí 22, tel. 24 21 28 44. For information on student hostels and other budget accommodation, head for the CKM (Youth Travel Bureau) office, Žitná 12, tel. 24 91 57 67. ČEDOK offices can reserve accommodation for you anywhere in the country.

AIRPORT (letiště)

Prague. Ruzyně International Airport lies about 20km (12 miles) northwest of Prague city centre. Facilities include 24-hour banks, left-luggage office, information desk, hotel reservation services, car rental agencies, post office, café, restaurants and duty-free shops. There are three options for transport into the city: municipal bus no. 119, which runs every 15 minutes from outside the terminal door to Dejvická Metro station, where you can take the Metro to anywhere in the city, journey time 35 to 60 minutes (there is a ticket machine beside the information desk – you will need two tickets, one each for bus and Metro); the Czech Airlines (ČSA) shuttle bus, which departs half-hourly between 7am and 7pm, and runs to the Airline Terminal, at Revoluční 25 (near náměstí Republiky Metro station), journey time 30 to 40 minutes (buy your ticket on the bus); and taxis, journey time about 30 minutes (for more information on taxis see p.136).

ČSA's domestic flights link Prague to Brno, Ostrava, Zlín, Karlovy Vary and Bratislava. The ČSA office in Prague is situated at Revoluční 1, tel. 24 80 61 11; for flight information tel. 24 81 51 03. British Airways is at Staroměstské náměstí 10, tel. 232 90 20. **117**

BICYCLE HIRE (půjčovna kol)

Cycling is a popular pastime in the Czech Republic, not just for fun, but as a regular means of transport. You will find bicycles for hire in all the areas frequented by tourists. Here are a few places to try – Prague: A Landa, Šumavská 33, Prague 6, tel. 253 99 82; Mipos, Za Humny 4, Prague 6, tel. 302 32 88; Karlovy Vary: American Express Travel Service (next to the Grand Hotel Pupp).

CAMPING and CARAVANNING

There are around 250 official campsites across the country, with pitches for both tents and caravans. Facilities are basic, but usually include showers, a kitchen block, and a shop. Most sites close down from October until March. Kartografie Praha (see Maps on p.128) publishes a map, *Autokempinky České republiky,* which lists campsites and includes telephone numbers, facilities, and opening times.

CAR HIRE (auto půjčovna) (See also DRIVING on p.122 and PLANNING YOUR BUDGET on p.131)

Renting a car is a good way of exploring the Czech Republic, giving you the freedom to travel at your own pace, and to explore areas that are inaccessible by public transport. Unfortunately, it is expensive compared to the UK and North America. Car hire agencies abound in Prague and the major cities and tourist resorts; local firms charge less than the big international chains. Rates vary greatly, so do shop around. It's usually best to book and pay for your car before you leave home, either directly through the UK office of an international rental company, or as part of a 'fly-drive' package deal. Check that the quoted rate includes collision damage waiver, theft protection, unlimited mileage, and local taxes; these are often not incorporated in the advertised rates, and can increase the total cost considerably.

Normally you must be over 21 to hire a car. You will need a full, valid driver's licence (EC model) which you have held for at least 12 months, your passport, and a major credit card – cash deposits are prohibitively large. Extra insurance is required if you plan to take the vehicle out of the Czech Republic (Slovakia excepted).

In Prague, some of the main car hire companies include: Hertz, Karlovo náměstí 28, Nové Město, tel. 29 78 36; Europcar/Interrent, Pařížská 28, Josefov, tel. 24 81 12 90; Avis, E. Krásnohorské 9, Staré Město, tel. 231 55 15; A Rent Car, Opletalova 33 (opposite railway station), tel. 24 22 98 48.

CLIMATE

The Czech Republic has a continental climate, with hot summers and cold, snowy winters, regularly disrupted by weather fronts moving through from the north and west. Although it is hot in July, it is the wettest month and February is the driest. Temperature and rainfall vary with altitude – it is wettest and coldest in the Giant Mountains, warmest and driest in the river basins of central and southern Bohemia, and refreshingly cool in summer in the hills of the Šumava.

The following chart indicates average minimum and maximum monthly temperatures in Prague:

		J	F	M	A	M	J	J	A	S	O	N	D
max.	°C	10	11	18	23	28	31	33	32	29	22	14	10
	°F	50	52	64	73	82	88	91	90	84	71	57	50
min.	°C	-13	-12	-8	-2	2	7	9	8	4	-2	-5	-10
	°F	9	10	18	28	36	45	48	46	39	28	23	14

Clothing. In summer lightweight cotton clothing is recommended, with a jacket or sweater for the evenings. Winter is very cold, with snow and ice, so take warm clothes, a good overcoat, and suitable footwear. Casual clothes are fine for most occasions, but a degree of formality is appropriate, certainly for visits to the opera or theatre, and at the more expensive restaurants in Prague, Brno, and the spa resorts. Use cloakroom facilities where these are provided.

COMMUNICATIONS

Post Offices (*pošta*). Post offices deal with mail, fax, telegram, telex and telephone services. Stamps (*známky*) are also available wherever postcards are sold. Most post offices are open 8am-6pm Monday to Friday; 8am-1pm Saturday. In Prague, the Head Post Office at Jindřišská 14 (just off Wenceslas Square) is open 24 hours. You may be asked to declare parcels at the Customs Clearance Office (*Pošta celnice*) at Post Office 121, Plzeňská 139, Prague 5.

Poste Restante/General Delivery. Mail should be addressed to you c/o Poste Restante, Jindřišská 14, Prague 1, Czech Republic. Pick up your mail at window 28 of the Head Post Office, but remember to take along your passport as identification.

Telegrams, **telexes and faxes**. These can be sent from post offices and from the business centres in major hotels.

Telephones (*telefon*). Local calls can be made from the public coin-operated telephones in the street and in bus and Metro stations. For long-distance and international calls use a telephone card (*telekarta*), or the post office telephone service. Give the clerk the number you want to dial, take your call in one of the booths, and pay afterwards.

You can also dial direct to an operator in your own country (see Direct numbers below), and make a charge card or reverse charge (collect) call. You can use most public phones – you will need a coin or phonecard, but these will be refunded after the call. For international directory enquiries dial 0149 (ask for an English speaker).

UK (BT)	0042 004401
UK (Mercury)	0042 004450
USA (AT&T)	0042 000101
USA (MCI)	0042 000112
USA (Sprint)	0042 087187
Canada	0042 000151
Australia	0042 006101
Germany	0042 004949

COMPLAINTS (*stížnost*)

Complaints should be addressed to the management of the hotel, restaurant or shop involved. If a polite inquiry fails to settle things, ask for the complaints book (*kniha přání a stížností*) – all businesses are required by law to keep one. If you are still dissatisfied, seek advice from tourist information (see p.135 for addresses).

CRIME
(See also EMERGENCIES on p.125 and POLICE on p.133)

In the Czech Republic, crime against foreigners, especially violent crime, is rare. The main problems are in Prague, where pickpockets work the tourist crowds in Old Town Square and on Charles Bridge, and theft from parked cars is common. You should take the usual precautions against theft – don't carry large amounts of cash, leave your valuables in the hotel safe, not in your room, and beware of pickpockets in crowded areas. Never leave your bags or valuables on view in a parked car – take them with you or lock them in the trunk. Any theft or loss must be reported immediately to the police in order to comply with your travel insurance. If your passport is lost or stolen, you should also inform your consulate.

CUSTOMS and ENTRY FORMALITIES

Visas. Citizens of the UK, Ireland and the USA need only a passport for visits of 90 days or less to the Czech Republic (the passport must be valid for at least 6 months after your date of entry). A visa, which is obtainable from the nearest Czech Embassy, is required by citizens of Canada, Australia, New Zealand and South Africa. (Note that visa regulations change from time to time, and you should always check the latest information through your travel agent before you leave.)

Currency restrictions. There are no restrictions on the amount of foreign currency that may be taken into or out of the Czech Republic. However, it is illegal for visitors to take more than 100 Kč in Czech currency out of the country without the authorization of the Czech National Bank.

Duty-free regulations. On arrival in the Czech Republic, you can bring into the country, duty-free: 250 cigarettes or 50 cigars or 250g tobacco; 1 litre of spirits or liqueurs, and 2 litres of wine; 50g of perfume or 250cc of eau de toilette. Any items, such as antiques, that might be considered part of the Czech heritage cannot be taken out of the country without special permission; more detailed information is available from antique shop owners or from the Customs Office, Sokolovská 22, Prague 8, tel. 24 22 21 86.

The Czech Republic is not part of the European Union. The customs allowances for travellers arriving in the UK from outside the EU are: 200 cigarettes or 50 cigars or 250g tobacco; 2 litres still table wine; 1 litre spirits or 2 litres fortified or sparkling wine; 60cc of perfume; 250cc of eau de toilette; other goods, including gifts and souvenirs, up to the value of £136.

For other countries, the customs allowances are: **Australia**: 250 cigarettes or 250g tobacco; 1litre alcohol. **Canada**: 200 cigarettes and 50 cigars and 400g tobacco; 1.1 litre spirits or wine or 8.5l beer. **New Zealand**: 200 cigarettes or 50 cigars or 250g tobacco; 4.5 litres wine or beer and 1.1 litre spirits. **South Africa**: 400 cigarettes and 50 cigars and 250g tobacco; 2 litres wine and 1 litre spirits. **USA**: 200 cigarettes and 100 cigars or a 'reasonable amount' of tobacco.

D

DRIVING

If you plan to bring your own vehicle into the Czech Republic, you will need: a valid driving licence; car registration papers; Green Card insurance; a national identity sticker (e.g. 'GB' or 'IRL'); a first-aid kit; and a red warning triangle for use in the event of a breakdown.

If you are driving someone else's vehicle, you must also have the owner's written permission.

Driving conditions. The minimum legal age for driving is 18; children under 12 are not allowed in the front passenger seat. Drive on the right, and pass on the left (except when there are two or more lanes in each direction, when either side is allowed). Trams must be passed on the right, but not while they have stopped to set down passengers. Seat-belts (both front and back) must be worn at all times, and alcohol is absolutely forbidden. Even a trace of alcohol in the driver's blood constitutes a serious offence. Speed limits are 110kph (68mph) on motorways, 90kph (56mph) on other roads, and 60kph (37mph) or 40kph (25mph) in towns and cities. The law is strictly enforced, and traffic police can levy on-the-spot fines; if you should have to pay a fine, always ask for a receipt (*účet*). When approaching junctions, priority is usually indicated by signs (see below) rather than road markings; at unmarked junctions, traffic on your right has priority. A tram which is to your left, but signalling that it is turning right and crossing your lane, has right of way.

There are motorways (toll-free) between Prague and Brno, Plzeň, and Poděbrady, and another under construction between Prague and Teplice. Most other main roads are simple two-lane highways. Bypasses are rare, and even Prague doesn't have a complete ring-road (yet); passing through towns can be time consuming. Level crossings are very common. Those on main roads have barriers, elsewhere there are only flashing lights, and on country roads there may only be a sign – here you have to stop and look for trains. Other hazards to beware of on country roads are tractors, cyclists and pedestrians.

Petrol (*benzín*). Most service stations are open from 6am-8 or 9pm. An increasing number, especially on major highways and near the major cities, are open 24 hours a day (they advertise themselves as *non-stop*). Fuel comes in four varieties: *special* (90 octane), *super* (96 octane), *naturál* (unleaded) and *nafta* (diesel). Pumps marked *samoobsluha* are self-service.

Parking. Most parking in central Prague is by permit only, and offenders will be clamped or towed away. In other towns, especially tourist towns, there will be signs directing you to a parking lot (*parkoviště*) near the town centre, where you will be charged a small fee. Some towns have 'pay and display' parking areas, marked by a blue sign with a 'P' and a picture of a meter. Buy a ticket from the machine and display it in the windscreen.

Traffic police. Czech traffic police are authorized to levy on-the-spot fines for traffic offences. They often set up speed traps on the edges of towns. They may also flag down traffic to make periodic checks on vehicles and documents, but as a tourist you will usually be waved on.

Breakdown. A reciprocal arrangement permits members of the AA and RAC to get help from the Czech Motoring Club. To contact their 'Yellow Angels' emergency breakdown service, dial 123 (preceded by the area code 02 if you are outside Prague). Any accident that involves injuries, or damage that amounts to more than 1,000 Kč, must be reported to the police.

Road signs. Most road signs are standard international pictographs. You will often see a sign consisting of a yellow diamond with a white border – this means that you are approaching a junction and the road you are on has right of way (the same sign with a black bar across it means you must give way). Speed limits are occasionally shown on a square blue sign with white figures, and direction signs can sometimes be a bit vague – be prepared for a few wrong turnings. Here are some written signs you may come across:

Benzínová stanice	Petrol station
Jednosměrný provoz	One way
Nevstupujte	No entry
Pozor	Attention
Pozor vlak	Beware of trains (at level crossing)
Pěší zóna	Pedestrian zone
Silnice se opravuje	Road under repair
Vchod/Vjezd	Way in
Východ	Way out
Zákaz parkování	No parking

Distance

Fluid measures

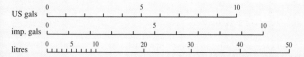

ELECTRIC CURRENT

220 V/50 Hz AC is standard. An adapter that fits continental-style two-pin sockets will be necessary; American 110 V appliances will also require a transformer.

EMBASSIES and CONSULATES

British Embassy: Thunovská 14, Prague 1, tel. 24 51 04 39.
Canadian Embassy: Mickiewiczova 6, Prague 6, tel. 24 31 11 08.
German Embassy: Vlašská 19, Prague 1, tel. 24 51 03 23.
South African Embassy: Ruská 65, Prague 10, tel. 67 31 11 14.
US Embassy: Tržiště 15, Prague 1, tel. 24 51 08 47.
Office hours are 8 or 8.30am-4 or 4.30pm.

EMERGENCIES

(See also EMBASSIES AND CONSULATES above, MEDICAL CARE on p.129 and POLICE on p.133)

Police	**158**
Ambulance	**155**
Fire	**150**

Although some emergency operators do speak English, it's best to have a Czech speaker dial these numbers for you.

125

ENVIRONMENTAL ISSUES

Prague suffers some of the worst traffic pollution in Europe, and its levels of sulphur dioxide are among the highest. Air quality is very poor in winter, and people affected with asthma or other respiratory complaints should try to avoid the Czech capital at this time of year.

GAY and LESBIAN TRAVELLERS

Homosexuality is not illegal in the Czech Republic, but even though Prague is fairly liberal, with a dozen or so gay bars or nightclubs, attitudes in the rural areas are still decidedly conservative.

GUIDES and TOURS (průvodce/cestování)
(See also TOURIST INFORMATION OFFICES on p.135)

There is a bewildering variety of guided tours on offer throughout the Czech Republic, from standard three-hour tours of Prague to day tours of historic castles, to river-boat cruises, hot-air balloon trips, sightseeing flights in light aircraft, and night-time ghost tours of Prague's Old Town. Travel agencies can provide you with details of the tours available in their region. Some agencies such as ČEDOK are also able to supply you with your personal English-speaking guide. For sightseeing around the castle in Prague, you can hire a guide directly at the Prague Castle Information Centre (see p.25).

Many of the castles, palaces and monasteries throughout the Czech Republic can only be visited on a guided tour (you don't have to book in advance, though – just turn up and join the next available one). The more popular destinations, such as Karlštejn Castle, offer tours in English and German (though you may have to wait for an hour or two during peak periods; the quietest times are before 10am and after 4pm); at other places the tour will be given in Czech, but there is usually a written English translation which you can read as you go – ask for the *anglický text*.

LANGUAGE

(See also Useful Expressions on the cover of this guide)

The national language is Czech. This is a Slavic language, related to Russian, but it uses the Roman rather than the Cyrillic alphabet. The most widely spoken foreign language is German. English is less widely known, but is more popular among younger people, and most tourist-related businesses have at least one English speaker.

The Czech alphabet is littered with diacritical marks (´, ˇ, and °), which make it appear formidably difficult, but once you learn a few basics you will find that each word is pronounced exactly as it is spelt. Here are a few tips on the pronunciation of the more difficult sounds:

t' like the *t* in **t**une	**č** like the *ch* in **ch**urch
ň like the *ny* in ca**ny**on	**ch** like the Scottish *ch* in lo**ch**
š like the *sh* in **sh**ine	**j** like the *y* in **y**ellow
ž like the *s* in plea**s**ure	**ř** like the *rs* in Pe**rs**ian
c like the *ts* in ca**ts**	

It is quite possible to enjoy a trip to the Czech Republic without knowing any Czech at all. All the same, it is polite to learn at least a few introductory phrases. Local people will welcome and encourage any attempt you make to use their own language. The Berlitz CZECH PHRASE BOOK AND DICTIONARY will cover most situations you are likely to encounter during your visit.

Do you speak English?	**Mluvíte anglicky?**
I don't speak Czech.	**Nemluvím česky.**
Hello/good day	**Ahoj/Dobrý den**
Goodbye	**Na shledanou**
Please/thank you	**Prosím/děkuji**
Excuse me	**Promiňte**
Yes/No	**Ano/Ne**

LOST PROPERTY (See also Embassies and Consulates on p.125, and Police on p.133)

Ask for advice from your hotel receptionist or the local Tourist Information Office before contacting the police. For items left behind on public transport, ask your hotel receptionist to telephone the bus or train station or taxi company. If you lose your passport, contact your embassy. The Lost Property Office in Prague (*Ztráty a nálezy*) is at Karoliny Světlé 5, Prague 1, tel. 24 23 50 85.

MAPS

Local publisher Kartografie Praha produces excellent town and city plans at scales of 1:15,000 and 1:10,000, and a motoring map of the Czech Republic at 1:500,000 (with historic castles, monasteries and other places of interest highlighted). They are available in bookshops and at news-stands in most tourist towns – look out for the yellow covers. Good hiking maps, at a scale of 1:50,000, are also available, showing the colour-coded walking trails that criss-cross the country. They are published in association with the Czech Touring Club (*Klub českých turistů*), and have green covers.

MEDIA

Radio. The BBC World Service and Voice of America broadcast in Prague, on FM 101.1 MHz and 106.2 MHz respectively, but elsewhere in the republic you will have to rely on short-wave reception.

Television. There are two state-run TV channels (ČT1 and ČT2) and two independent channels broadcasting in Czech, and also a choice of German, Austrian, Slovakian and Polish channels, depending on which part of the country you are in. ČT2 broadcasts Euronews in English from 8-8.45am and 12-12.30pm weekdays (7-8am Saturday and Sunday), and occasionally shows undubbed English-language films (with Czech subtitles). Most hotels also have satellite channels, usually including the English-language Eurosport and CNN.

Newspapers (*noviny*). Local English-language publications include the weekly *Prague Post*, with news, features, restaurant reviews and entertainment listings. *Velvet* magazine caters for expatriates and tourists, and offers reviews and listings. The *Guardian International* and the *International Herald Tribune* are available at news-stands in central Prague; outside the capital, English-language papers are rare. German papers can be found in the more popular tourist towns.

MEDICAL CARE

The UK has a reciprocal arrangement with the Czech Republic that allows British citizens to receive free medical treatment in Czech hospitals. This applies only to urgently needed treatment, and any prescribed medicines or non-emergency care will have to be paid for. You will need to show your passport to claim free treatment.

Despite this arrangement, you should not leave home without an adequate insurance policy, preferably one that includes cover for an emergency flight home in the event of serious injury or illness. Your travel agent, bank, building society or insurance broker can provide a comprehensive policy which will cover not only medical costs, but also theft or loss of money and possessions, delayed or cancelled flights, and so on.

There are a number of private clinics in Prague where you can consult English-speaking doctors (though you will have to pay for these services). A 24-hour private medical service for foreigners is available at Karlovo náměstí 32, Prague 2, tel. 24 91 48 24.

For minor ailments, the local pharmacy (*lékárna*) should be able to help. Pharmacies are usually open during normal shopping hours. After hours, at least one per town remains open all night; its location is posted in the window of all other pharmacies. In Prague, there is a 24-hour pharmacy situated at Na příkopě 7, Prague 1 (Old Town), tel. 24 21 02 29. If you are taking prescription medicines, bring along an adequate supply, as the equivalent may be difficult to obtain or unavailable in the Czech Republic.

Vaccinations. There are no compulsory immunization requirements for entry into the Czech Republic.

MONEY MATTERS

Currency. The unit of currency is the Czech crown (*Koruna česká*), usually shortened to Kč, which is divided into 100 heller (*haléř*).

Coins: 10, 20, 50 heller, 1, 2, 5, 10, 20 and 50 Kč.

Notes: 20, 50, 100, 200, 500, 1000, and 5000 Kč.

Since the break-up of Czechoslovakia in 1993, the Czech and Slovak republics have had separate currencies. The old Czechoslovak crown (*Koruna československa*) is no longer legal tender in either country.

Banks and currency exchange offices (*banka*; *směnárna*). Banks are open 8am-noon and 1-5pm Monday to Friday; exchange offices are usually open late in the evening and at weekends; some in Prague are open 24 hours. Best rates for changing currency and traveller's cheques are in the major banks; try the Československá Obchodní Banka and the Komerční Banka. Commission is around 1-3%, with a minimum charge of around 50 Kč. Exchange booths may be open longer hours, but they charge huge commissions of 5-10%.

Traveller's cheques. These are usually accepted by middle and upper grade hotels, and by the banks mentioned above. Hotels offer a poor rate of exchange, while banks charge a commission of around 1-3%. The best places to change traveller's cheques are American Express and Thomas Cook offices, who charge no commission for changing their own cheques into Czech crowns. Take your passport when cashing traveller's cheques. The American Express and Thomas Cook offices in Prague are on Wenceslas Square (open 9am-7pm daily in summer; Amex closes at 3pm weekends). American Express offices can also be found in Karlovy Vary and in Bratislava.

Credit cards. Major credit and charge cards are accepted in the more expensive hotels and restaurants in the larger towns and cities, and by tourist shops, travel agencies and car hire firms, but always ask first. Visa and Access/Mastercard can also be used in banks to obtain cash advances, and in automatic teller machines to withdraw cash (Czech crowns only, PIN required). A credit card and an ATM **130** is the fastest and easiest way of getting cash in the Czech Republic.

Planning your budget

To give you an idea of what to expect, here is a list of prices in Czech crowns (Kč). These can only be regarded as approximate, as inflation continues to push prices up.

Airport transfer. From Prague airport to city centre. Municipal bus and Metro, 20 Kč; ČSA shuttle bus, 30 Kč; taxi fare is about 350 Kč.

Bicycle hire. Typical rates are 70 Kč an hour, 340 Kč a day.

Camping. About 60 to 100 Kč a night for a tent, plus 70 Kč per person. Car 90 Kč, caravan 90 Kč, motor caravan 170 Kč.

Car hire. Local rates for a Škoda Favorit, including CDW and local taxes, are 930 Kč a day plus 5.70 Kč per km, or 8,880 Kč a week with unlimited mileage. Pre-booked in the UK through a major international firm, an Opel Corsa costs around £290 a week including unlimited mileage, CDW and tax. Petrol costs around 19-20 Kč a litre.

Entertainment. Prague opera or theatre 300-700 Kč, concert 50-500 Kč, cinema 40-50 Kč.

Excursions. 2- or 3-hour guided tours of Prague, 290-450 Kč. Day trip from Prague to Karlštejn Castle, 900-1,400 Kč. 'Prague by Night' boat trip, dinner included, 1,600 Kč.

Hotels (double room with bath, including breakfast). Outside Prague and Karlovy Vary: 1-star 300-500 Kč; 2-star 500-1,000 Kč; 3-star 1,000-2,000 Kč; 4-star over 2,000 Kč. In central Prague all hotels are much more expensive – 3-star 2,000-3,000 Kč; 5-star over 6,000 Kč.

Meals and drinks. Lunch/dinner for two in a good restaurant, 300-800 Kč; cup of coffee, 20 Kč; 0.5l glass of beer, 10-20 Kč; glass of wine 35 Kč; can of soft drink, 10-20 Kč.

Photography and video. 36-exposure colour print film (excluding printing and processing), 135 Kč; 36-exposure colour slide film (excluding processing), 170 Kč; 120-minute Hi-8 video cassette, 630 Kč. (From photo shop in Prague; more expensive elsewhere.)

Public transport in Prague. Flat fare, 6 Kč; tourist pass, valid on Metro, trams and buses: 1 day, 50 Kč; 2 days, 85 Kč; 3 days, 110 Kč; 4 days, 135 Kč; 5 days, 170 Kč.

Sightseeing. Prague Castle, combined ticket for St Vitus Cathedral, Royal Palace and Basilica of St George, 80 Kč; Prague Town Hall tower, 20 Kč; State Jewish Museum, 270 Kč; Český Krumlov Castle, 70 Kč; Hluboká Castle, 40 Kč.

Taxis. In Prague, the legal rate is 10 Kč flag-fall plus 12 Kč per km.

OPENING HOURS
(See also Public Holidays on p.133)

Banks. 8am-12 noon and 1-5pm, Monday to Friday.

Currency exchange offices. 8am-8pm daily, some in Prague open 24 hours.

Museums and art galleries. Most state-owned castles, museums and galleries are open 9am-6pm, closed Monday.

Post offices. 8am to 6pm Monday to Friday, 8am to 1pm Saturday.

Shops. 8am-5pm Monday to Friday, 8am-12 noon Saturday.

Some useful signs to know: *Otevřeno* (open); *Zavřeno* (closed); *hodiny/hod.* (hours).

P

PHOTOGRAPHY (*fotografie*)

Major brands of film are available throughout the Czech Republic, but they are more expensive than in the UK, so stock up before you leave. Protect your film from the effects of heat, and never leave a camera or film lying in direct sunlight. Photography is forbidden in many museums, churches and cathedrals, so always check before snapping away. If you want to take photos of the local people, it is polite to ask permission first. For detailed information on how to get the most out of holiday photographs, see the Berlitz-Nikon Pocket Guide to Travel Photography (available in the UK only).

Video. It is usually forbidden to use a camcorder inside many tourist sights. Spare video cassettes can be bought at photo shops.

POLICE (*policie*)
(See also EMERGENCIES on p.125)

There are two kinds of police in the Czech Republic. The state police have khaki uniforms and carry guns, and are the ones who patrol the highways. If you have been robbed, however, and need to get a report for insurance purposes, you need to go to the nearest office of the municipal police, who have black uniforms and are controlled by the local authorities. Police officers rarely speak English, so you should take along an interpreter. In Prague, the British Embassy will give you a letter in Czech, asking for a report, to take to the Police HQ, which is at Konviktská 14 in the Old Town, tel. 24 13 11 11. If you can speak Czech, or can get someone to speak for you, telephone the police in an emergency (in Prague) by dialling 158.

PUBLIC HOLIDAYS

1 January	*Nový rok*	New Year's Day
1 May	*Svátek práce*	May Day
8 May	*Vítěztví nad fašismem*	Victory over Fascism (Liberation Day)
5 July	*Slovanští věrozvěsti sv. Cyril a Metoděj*	St Cyril and St Methodius Day
6 July	*Výročí úmrtí Jana Husa*	Anniversary of Jan Hus's death
28 October	*První československá republika*	Independence Day (founding of first Czechoslovak Republic)
24 December	*Štědrý den*	Christmas Eve
25-26 December	*Svátek vánoční*	Christmas and Boxing Day
Movable date	*Velikonoční pondělí*	Easter Monday

Are you open tomorrow?   **Máte zítra otevřeno?**   **133**

R

RELIGION

Around 40% of Czechs are Roman Catholic. There are significant minorities of Protestant and Orthodox Christians, and a small Jewish community in Prague. About 40% of Czechs profess to be atheist.

Roman Catholic Mass is said at 7am each day in Prague's St Vitus Cathedral. Divine Service is held in the Old-New Synagogue at 8am on weekdays, and 9am on Saturday. Prague Christian Fellowship holds services in English at 6pm on Sundays (except the first Sunday in the month), at the YMCA, Na poříčí 12, Prague 1.

T

TIME DIFFERENCES

The Czech Republic is on Central European time (GMT + 1), with daylight saving time (GMT + 2) in operation from the end of March until the end of September. The following table shows the time difference in various cities in **summer**.

New York	London	**Prague**	Sydney	Los Angeles
6am	11am	**noon**	8pm	3am

TIPPING

Tipping is now common practice in tourist hotels and restaurants. The chart below will give you some guidelines.

Hotel porter, per bag	10 Kč
Hotel maid, per week	50 Kč
Cloakroom (hat check) attendant	2 Kč
Waiter	10-15%
Taxi driver	round up the fare
Tour guide	50 Kč
Theatre usher	5-10 Kč

TOILETS/RESTROOMS (toalety)

Public facilities are found in restaurants, railway and Metro stations, museums, galleries and other tourist attractions. They are usually signposted 'WC', with *Muži* or *Páni* for men and *Ženy* or *Dámy* for women. There is usually a small fee of 1 or 2 Kč.

TOURIST INFORMATION OFFICES (cestovní kancelář)

You can obtain brochures and general tourist information on the Czech Republic from the Czech Tourist Authority. The former state-run ČEDOK now functions as a commercial travel agency, and its overseas offices no longer provide general tourist information, though it can organize tours, arrange accommodation and provide other tourist services.

There are tourist information desks at Prague's airport and railway station, and several others in the city centre. The principal city centre offices are Prague Information Service (PIS) at Na příkopě 20 and Staroměstské náměstí 1 (entrance to Old Town Hall, open 9am-7pm, 6pm weekends), tel. 187; and ČEDOK at Na příkopě 18, tel. 24 19 76 43. For information about the rest of the country, visit the Czech Tourist Authority (*Česká centrála cestovního ruchu*) at Národní 37, tel. 24 21 14 58 (open 10am-6pm daily).

You can obtain information about the Czech Republic before you leave home, by contacting one of the offices below.

Austria: Czech Tourist Authority, Herrengasse 17, 1010 Wien, tel. (01) 535 2361.

Germany: Czech Tourist Authority, Leipzigerstrasse 60, D10117 Berlin, tel. (030) 200 4770.

UK: Czech Tourist Authority, c/o Embassy of the Czech Republic, 30 Kensington Palace Gardens, London W8 4QY, tel. (0171) 243 1115.

ČEDOK, 49 Southwark Street, London SE1 1RU, tel. (0171) 378 6009, fax 403 2321.

USA: ČEDOK, Suite 1902, 10 E. 40th Street, New York, NY10016, tel. (212) 689 9720, fax 481 0579.

TRANSPORT

City transport. Prague has an integrated public transport system, including Metro, trams and buses. Single tickets (*jízdenka*) can be bought from kiosks and newsagents, or from machines inside Metro stations (exact fare only). Tickets must be validated before use: on buses and trams you punch your ticket using a little machine by the door – put the ticket in and pull towards you. A new ticket is needed for each journey. On the Metro you put your ticket in a machine at the station entrance. The ticket is valid for 60 minutes, during which time you can make as many Metro journeys and transfers as you like. Tourist tickets are also available. These are valid for 1 to 5 days, do not need to be stamped, and can be used on Metro, bus and tram. Other Czech cities like Brno and Hradec Králové have transport systems that are run along the same lines, but without the Metro service.

Výstup/Východ	exit
Vstup/Vchod	entrance
Přestup	connection
Směr	direction, i.e. towards
Stanice	station

Long-distance buses. There is a good network of long-distance bus routes in the Czech Republic, run mostly by the Czech Bus Service (ČAD or ČSAD). The bus is usually faster and cheaper than the train. Comprehensive route maps and timetables can be found at main bus stations; buy your ticket at the station before you board the bus. In Prague, most long-distance international and domestic buses leave from Florenc bus station (next to Florenc Metro station). Booking for international buses can be made at most travel agents; for domestic trips you have to go to the station. For timetable information in Prague, tel. 24 21 10 60 (6am-8pm Monday to Friday).

Taxis. Taxis are available in all cities and large towns. Prague has a problem with crooked taxi drivers, especially on the route between the airport and city centre. Make sure the driver uses the meter, and ask him what the fare will be before you get in. At the end of the trip, ask for a receipt (say *'Účet, prosím'*), especially if the fare seems to be excessive. It's best to order a taxi by phone – there are a number of reliable new taxi companies in Prague. Try AAA Taxi, tel. 33 99 (English spoken); or ProfiTaxi, tel. 61 04 55 55.

Trains. The Czech Republic has one of Europe's cheapest and most extensive rail networks; unfortunately it is also one of the slowest. The fastest trains are called *expres* or *rychlík,* but you have to make a reservation for these trains at least an hour before departure time (they are marked with an 'R' in the timetable). For shorter journeys, up to 120km (74 miles) (e.g. Prague to Plzeň), you can buy a ticket from a coin-operated machine. The Eurotrain Czech Explorer Pass gives one week's unlimited train travel within the Czech Republic. It is available to European residents under 26, holders of ISIC cards (whatever age), and teachers and their spouses and children. They must be bought *before* you come to the Czech Republic. The Inter-Rail and Inter-Rail 26+ Passes are also valid on Czech railways.

TRAVELLING TO THE CZECH REPUBLIC

By air

Scheduled flights. Prague's Ruzyně International Airport is well served by direct scheduled flights from major European and North American cities. The national carrier, Czech Airlines (ČSA), and British Airways both have daily direct flights from London to Prague. For details of flights, contact Czech Airlines, tel. (0171) 255 1898; or British Airways, tel. (0181) 897 4000 (London area) or 01345 222111 (rest of UK). ČSA also flies direct from New York and Montreal to Prague several times a week.

Charter flights and package tours. A wide range of package tours from the UK and North America to the Czech Republic is available, from short city breaks in Prague to week-long tours of the whole country. The price usually includes a return flight to Prague, airport transfer, and accommodation with breakfast. Further information and booking details are available from your travel agent.

By road
(See also DRIVING on p.122)

The most direct overland route from London to the Czech Republic is through Belgium and Germany, taking the E50 route via Frankfurt and Nuremberg, and entering the country at Waidhaus-Rozvadov. This border crossing is open 24 hours a day. It can be very busy, and long queues build up at weekends and holidays. Prague is 1,062km (660 miles) from Ostend and 1,158km (720 miles) from Calais.

By rail
The fastest rail link from London to Prague takes around 20 hours, changing at Brussels and Köln. A slightly longer route (22 hours) takes the Eurostar service to Paris, changing in Paris and Köln. For details, contact British Rail at London Victoria, tel. (0171) 834 2345.

TRAVELLERS WITH DISABILITIES
(See also ENVIRONMENTAL ISSUES on p.126)

Provision for disabled travellers in the Czech Republic is generally poor or non-existent, but the situation is changing all the time. Public transport is not wheelchair accessible, except for a few trains, but the more modern hotels, especially those built in the last five years, often have a few rooms designed for wheelchair travellers. A useful contact address is the Czech Association of Persons with Disabilities, Karlínské náměstí 12, Prague 8, tel. 24 21 59 15 (open 8am-4pm).

WATER
Tap water is safe to drink throughout the Czech Republic. Bottled mineral water, both still and sparkling, is widely available; *Dobrá voda* (literally 'good water') is one of the most popular brands.

WEIGHTS and MEASURES
The Czech Republic uses the metric system. For fluid and distance measures, see p.125.

Length

cm / inches scale from 0 to 30 cm / 0 to 12 inches

metres / ft/yd scale from 0 to 2 m / 0 to 2 yd

Weight

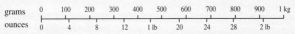

grams / ounces scale from 0 to 1 kg / 0 to 2 lb

Temperature

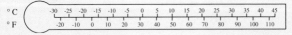

°C scale from -30 to 45 / °F scale from -20 to 110

WOMEN TRAVELLERS

Women travelling alone will encounter few problems in the Czech Republic. You should avoid hitch-hiking, and be aware that certain areas near the German border, especially the road between Děčín and Hřensko in the České Švýcarsko, are pick-up zones for prostitutes.

Y

YOUTH HOSTELS
(See also ACCOMMODATION on p.116)

There are several official youth hostels in the Czech Republic run by the Youth Travel Office CKM, which is affiliated to the IHYF. You don't need to be a member to use these hostels, but members do get significant price reductions. In Prague, the Strahov Hostel Estec at Vaníčkova 5/blok 5, Prague 6, tel. (02) 52 73 44, fax 52 73 43, is open all year round. Further information and a list of hostels world-wide are available from the International Youth Hostel Federation (IYHF), 9 Guessens Road, Welwyn Garden City, Herts AL8 6QW, United Kingdom, tel. (01707) 332 487.

Index

Where there is more than one set of references, the one in **bold** refers to the main entry. Numbers in *italic* refer to an illustration.

141

143

Other Berlitz titles include:

Africa
Kenya
Morocco
South Africa
Tunisia

Asia, Middle East
Bali and Lombok
China
Egypt
Hong Kong
India
Indonesia
Israel
Japan
Malaysia
Singapore
Sri Lanka
Taiwan
Thailand

Australasia
Australia
New Zealand
Sydney

Austria, Switzerland
Austrian Tyrol
Switzerland
Vienna

**Belgium,
The Netherlands**
Amsterdam
Bruges and Ghent
Brussels

British Isles
Channel Islands
Dublin
Edinburgh
Ireland
London
Scotland

**Caribbean,
Latin America**
Bahamas
Bermuda
Cancún and Cozumel
Caribbean
Cuba

French West Indies
Jamaica
Mexico
Mexico City/Acapulco
Puerto Rico
Rio de Janeiro
Southern Caribbean
Virgin Islands

**Central and
Eastern Europe**
Budapest
Moscow and
St Petersburg
Prague

France
Brittany
Châteaux of the Loire
Côte d'Azur
Dordogne
Euro Disney Resort
France
Normandy
Paris
Provence

Germany
Berlin
Munich
Rhine Valley

**Greece, Cyprus
and Turkey**
Athens
Corfu
Crete
Cyprus
Greek Islands
Istanbul
Rhodes
Turkey

Italy and Malta
Florence
Italy
Malta
Milan and the Lakes
Naples
Rome
Sicily
Venice

North America
Alaska Cruise Guide
Boston
California
Canada
Disneyland and the
Theme Parks of
Southern California
Florida
Hawaii
Los Angeles
New Orleans
New York
San Francisco
USA
Walt Disney World
and Orlando
Washington

Portugal
Algarve
Lisbon
Madeira
Portugal

Scandinavia
Copenhagen
Helsinki
Oslo and Bergen
Stockholm
Sweden

Spain
Barcelona
Canary Islands
Costa Blanca
Costa del Sol
Costa Dorada and
Tarragona
Ibiza and Formentera
Madrid
Mallorca and Menorca
Spain

IN PREPARATION
Channel Hopper's Wine
Guide (will be available
in the UK)

144